ABOUT THE AUTHOR

Ruth Stenerson is uniquely qualified to write this book. She has a master's degree in English from the University of North Dakota, Grand Forks, and is presently an associate professor of English at Bemidji State University (BSU) in Bemidji, Minnesota. Articles by Ruth have appeared in various Christian journals and devotional books. Ruth's work has also been published in *Minnesota English Journal*. She wrote and compiled a *Handbook for the Bible as Literature* which is used as the text for a course in the Bible as literature which she teaches at BSU.

A single herself, Ruth Stenerson has a special sensitivity to the needs and concerns of single people. She is active in her home congregation and also is involved in campus ministry at BSU.

Bible Readings
FOR
SINGLES

Bible Readings

FOR
SINGLES

·

Ruth Stenerson

AUGSBURG Publishing House
Minneapolis, Minnesota 55415

BIBLE READINGS FOR SINGLES

Copyright © 1980 Augsburg Publishing House

Library of Congress Catalog Card No. 80-65543

International Standard Book No. 0-8066-1788-8

Scripture quotations unless otherwise noted are from the Good News Bible, Today's English Version: copyright © American Bible Society 1966, 1971, 1976. Used by permission.

Scripture quotations marked NIV are from the Holy Bible: New International Version. Copyright 1978 by the New York International Bible Society. Used by permission of Zondervan Bible Publishers.

The hymn stanza on page 24 is used by permission of the Board of Publication, Lutheran Church in America.

Quotations from the poems "Revelation" (p. 40) and "Mending Wall" (p. 94) are from *The Poetry of Robert Frost* edited by Edward Connery Lathem. Copyright 1930, 1934, 1939, © 1969 by Holt, Rinehart and Winston. Copyright © 1958, 1962 by Robert Frost. Copyright © 1967 by Lesley Frost Ballantine. Reprinted by permission of Holt, Rinehart and Winston, Publishers.

*To the friends, no matter what
their marital status, who have
caused me to perceive God's
love as I have experienced theirs*

PREFACE

Millions of Americans live alone: some have never married; others by death of marriage or mate again live as singles. Recent census estimates report that one in every five American households consists of just one person. Numbers of men and women living alone have more than doubled since 1970.

Until recently in our society, "failure" to marry was an embarrassing state of affairs—even unmarried persons themselves refrained from talking about being single, as if it were somehow a shameful thing. Older relatives prodded them with continual questions about when they planned to marry: "Is there anyone in sight?" Fortunately, there is a healthier realization today that, as St. Paul knew long ago, marriage is not for everyone.

Increasing numbers of people live alone or as single adults as a result of divorce. Their interests and needs are similar in many ways to those of the unmarried, as are those of people whose marriage has been broken by death.

The church has traditionally assumed that a congregation is made up of family units. Church activities and publications, even sermons, often are directed exclusively to families. This is, we can be sure, due more to a lack of awareness of the numbers of people who live alone than to deliberate neglect. In reality, a large proportion of any congregation is made up of people who are not living in a nuclear family. Although the church today is becoming more conscious of this fact, those of us who live as singles need to do more speaking out about the needs we have. We must help each other meet our spiritual, social, and physical needs.

The devotional writings in this book are intended for all those for whom the events of their lives have resulted in their living alone. They have grown out of my own life as a single. I have been richly blessed in my friends, both single and married. I can look at living alone in a positive way, as the challenge it is, because I have known many who make the single life-style work well in their lives. Living alone can be a challenge and a satisfaction.

The most important part of each page is the selection from the Scriptures. Please read the selections before you read the paragraphs that follow them. The prayers are intended to be only a beginning to lead you into your own personal prayer. I hope this book can come to be a friend because it expresses what is meaningful to you.

■ THE GIFT OF SINGLENESS

1 Cor. 7:7-17: "Actually I would prefer that all of you were as I am; but each one has a special gift from God, one person this gift, another one that gift" (v. 7).

Paul is speaking of being married or single when he here states his preference. To him it seems desirable to be single, but the conclusion he comes to is, "Each one should go on living according to the Lord's gift to him."

Down through the centuries in the Christian church the idea that singleness is a gift from God has been readily accepted for those who joined a religious order. The idea that singleness for others might be a gift from God has seldom entered people's minds. The person who is single, to the minds of the majority, is in an unnatural state and should be doing everything in his or her power to get out of that situation. This attitude is changing. But do even many of us who are single see our gift as one to be desired? Or is it a burden, encouraging us to worry about our futures and to think less of ourselves? If we find our singleness a burden, perhaps we need to remind ourselves that being married is at times a burden too, even in a happy marriage.

There are advantages to the single life. If our attitude is right, God can help us see that it is a special gift from him.

I must confess, Lord, that there are times I do not see my life as a single, living alone, as a special gift from you. Open my eyes and help me rejoice in your gift to me. Amen.

Before you go to bed tonight, make a list of at least three ways in which your single life-style can be considered a gift to be accepted with contentment.

■ THE JEWEL OF CONTENTMENT

Phil. 4:4-13: "For I have learned to be content whatever the circumstances" (v. 11 NIV).

Some people choose the single life and find contentment in it. Others are single or live alone for lack of alternatives. Many older people are alone because they took on—or were left with—responsibilities for care of elderly family members. Some of us are single now but will not remain so in the future. No doubt those among us who are least content are those for whom singleness is an unwanted disappointment or a condition resulting from the death of a mate or a broken marriage.

It is significant that Paul does not speak of contentment as a state of mind that comes naturally. He *learned* to be content; he had experiences which taught him contentment.

Few people are content all the time. If there are times when our single life-style is a source of discontent, we can remember that married people have their times of discontent as well. As singles know, those who are married at times express jealousy or resentment of the freedom they believe singles have.

Contentment with our way of life is a lesson God will help us learn. When it comes from his hand, we know he can use it to serve a positive purpose in our lives.

Teach me, O Lord, to be content in whatever state you want me to be. Give me a divine discontent to let me know when I am not where you want me. Amen.

Out of your personal reasons for contentment, formulate a prayer. Write it down and keep it in this book for use on days when you are tempted to be discontented.

■ WHEN PEOPLE USE PEOPLE

Gen. 16:1-6: "Why don't you sleep with my slave girl? Perhaps she can have a child for me" (v. 2).

The story of how Sarah used Hagar for her own purposes and then cast her off is not a pretty one. The results are seldom good when we deliberately use other people to fulfill our own needs while disregarding their well-being and personhood. One can understand why Sarah found it hard to have faith that God could accomplish his plan to give Abraham many descendants without her help in the matter, but one can lose much respect for Sarah for her willingness to cast out Hagar and her baby when Sarah herself was responsible for what had happened.

Because we who live as singles have the same social needs as others, we too can be tempted to use people for our own advantage, not because we enjoy them and wish to share life with them, but because they satisfy some need in us. Our relationships with friends do satisfy our needs, but with them we must take care to be involved in both giving and receiving. How easy to reach out to others without ever realizing what our motives are! Indeed, if we think about it, we may find that we are even trying to use God for our own purposes.

My Lord, I praise you for friends who add so much richness to my life. Keep me from unconsciously using them for my own advantage. Amen.

Plan a simple but enjoyable occasion to share with a friend to express your gratitude for what this friend means to you in your life.

◼ LIVING WITH OUR DECISIONS

Gen. 16:1-16: "Then Sarai said to Abraham, 'It's your fault that Hagar despises me'" (v. 5).

Sarah was a manager. If an event she anticipated did not happen when she expected it, Sarah went into action. This was true when God promised her and her husband an heir in their old age. Rather than wait upon God, Sarah recommended the usual custom for circumventing the barrenness of a wife. She told Abraham to take her servant as a mistress. It was Sarah's suggestion, Sarah's idea: one gets the impression that her word was Abraham's command. Her plan worked. Hagar had a son; Abraham had a descendant. Then, feeling her womanhood belittled, Sarah could no longer live with what she had brought about and wanted Hagar cast out.

We who live as singles are constantly faced with the need to make decisions. If we make bad decisions, some might be reversible. Others, like Sarah's, are not. It takes grace to live with the result of a bad decision without causing others to bear the penalty for it. Happiness for us and for others is more likely if we accept what is irreversible in our decisions and, by God's strength, make the best of it.

 Lord, keep me from poorly thought out decisions. When I do make them, keep me from blaming the consequences on someone else. Amen.

When faced with important decisions, make it a custom to list the pros and cons in writing as an aid in examining the decision objectively.

◼ HAGAR, THE WRONGED ONE

Gen. 21:1-21: "Then God opened her eyes, and she saw a well" (v. 19).

Hagar is not the only single person to be left with the care of a child and a heartache along with it. Taken from her Egyptian homeland, then, with her child, thrown off like a used appliance, Hagar's prospects were not very bright. She watched her son, Ishmael, gradually dehydrate in the desert heat, and she was helpless. Abraham, although fond of Ishmael, nevertheless yielded to Sarah's jealousy, and there was no one on Hagar's side—no one, that is, but God. But that was enough. God, hearing Ishmael's cries, enabled Hagar to see the provision for their needs: he opened her eyes and she saw a well of water. Ishmael grew up to have as many sons as were born in the second generation of Isaac's offspring.

The point at which God will meet us in our need is beyond our ability to predict. Nor can we know through whom he will choose to deal with us. There are two things this story suggests: he meets us as a result of prayer, and he is likely to meet us at the point of our greatest need. The slave girl had her eyes opened to see her need supplied, and by a god not linked to her own people. Our God meets us in our needs too, but not always in the way we expect.

Prayer Suggestion: In your prayer tell God what you consider your greatest need; the point where you yearn to have him meet you in your life today.

Do you know a parent who has serious concerns about her or his ability to care for a child? Find some way today to express your concern and support for that parent.

■ ALONE OR LONELY?

Gen. 37:2-24: "So they hated him even more because of his dreams and because of what he said about them" (v. 8).

A very real difference exists between loneliness and aloneness. As singles we probably experience more aloneness than do those who live in family groupings, but we have no necessary monopoly on loneliness. There are many evidences in both our experience and in the Bible of people who lived within family situations, yet who knew a loneliness that must have been hard to bear. Imagine the loneliness of Joseph within that family of brothers who hated him, even if it was his own tactlessness that was partly to blame. Or the loneliness of Samson when he had lost his strength, or that of Saul when both Samuel and God had deserted him. Joshua must have felt loneliness when he took over the leadership of the Hebrews knowing they expected the same kind of miracle-filled rule from him that they had experienced under Moses.

Aloneness can be used creatively: it can enrich us and cause us to develop our inner resources. Loneliness is another matter; it is something all human beings experience, whether living in or out of a family setting. We need to be able to differentiate between the two and seek to use each constructively.

 Lord, I am grateful that with your presence in my life I am never entirely alone, nor need I feel really lonely. Amen.

At what times of day do you find aloneness constructive and desirable? When do you find it liable to turn into loneliness? Could you change your schedule in any way that would make loneliness less likely to take over?

■ THE LONELINESS OF SUCCESS

Gen. 41:25-45: "He gave Joseph the Egyptian name Zaphenath Paneah, and he gave him a wife, Asenath, the daughter of Potiphera, a priest in the city of Heliopolis" (v. 45).

Apart from his native culture, bound to a foreign state, handed a wife from a family of a priest of a different religion, Joseph knew the loneliness of being a stranger in a far-off land. And, as an official of the Egyptian government, he was probably envied and resented by others and knew another kind of loneliness, a loneliness that can come from success. Yet in no instance does he complain.

Because singles often have a freedom of choice that permits dedication to a job with fewer distractions or obligations, many may experience jealousy or resentment from others along with success at their job. Because responsibilities and ties in even the closest of families are sometimes burdensome, the ones who feel these burdens may resent or envy the freedom singles have in their choices and movements. Loneliness can be a result of success as well as of failure. Yet to seek to avoid success is, for singles and married alike, to be content to be less than our best. But we can find ways to be helpful and generous in our work that can reduce a negative response from others.

Help me, O Lord, not to shut anyone behind a wall of loneliness because he or she is more successful than I. Amen.

Think about some person you know whose position of leadership may cause him loneliness. In some way today extend to him or her a specific act of friendship or an encouraging greeting.

■ THE TREASURE OF FRIENDSHIP

1 Sam. 20:16-42: "God be with you. The Lord will make sure that you and I, and your descendants and mine, will forever keep the sacred promise we have made to each other" (v. 42).

David and Jonathan's names have long been linked as a reminder of the beauty and supportiveness of close friendships. Jonathan, who recognized his father's psychotic fear of David, maintained both his loyalty to his father's house and his loyalty to his friend.

Inevitably there have been those in our modern day who have insisted that the relationship between David and Jonathan was a homosexual one. I think especially those of us who are singles need to raise a protest here. Our society has become so obsessed with sex that it is difficult for friends of the same sex to show any affection or enduring loyalty to each other without leaving themselves open to gossip. Above all, to touch a friend is suspect.

It is sad if friends must refrain from offering each other affection and support because of this kind of suspicion. There seem no limits to the suggestive behavior that can be displayed between those of opposite sex, but any warmth and enduring loyalty of same-sex friends becomes suspect. We cannot let friendship be perverted by constant fear of such criticism.

Lord, we believe the love of human friends for each other is a reflection in our lives of your great and abiding friendship for us. Help us to be true friends to others. Amen.

Spend a little time today thinking of pressures placed on individuals by society which reduce our effectiveness in meeting the friendship needs of others.

■ THE STILL SMALL VOICE

1 Kings 19:1-12: ". . . but the Lord was not in the fire; and after the fire a still small voice" (v. 12 KJV).

How reassuring to know that it is in the "still small voice" rather than in the tumult of earthquake that God speaks to us! While many singles are busy in the active hubbub of life, many others are tied to the more quiet routines of everyday-ness. Yet, if that is our lot, we are no less likely to hear the still small voice than those whose lives are more dramatic. Maybe it is even harder for them to sort out the noises and identify the voice.

Elijah's life had been full of turmoil in the story that precedes our text. Yet it was while he was alone, secluded in the desert and on the mountain, that the gentle whisper could be heard. Then, when Elijah had listened, God sent him back into the furor with renewed strength.

The listening both followed and was followed by obedience. We will find that too. When we come with an obedient heart to the Word, the Spirit opens that Word to us, and we can go on in our lives strengthened to be obedient in what the day brings us. Sometimes we can identify the voice in a new certainty in our beings about what we are to do next or how we are to face the day's problems and responsibilities.

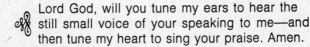 Lord God, will you tune my ears to hear the still small voice of your speaking to me—and then tune my heart to sing your praise. Amen.

Take a few extra minutes to meditate on times and events in your life in which you were most aware of the "still small voice." What did those times mean in your life?

■ THE ONLY ONE LEFT

1 Kings 19:13-21: "I am the only one left—and they are trying to kill me" (v. 14).

How easy to believe, as Elijah does here, that "I am the only one left." Especially for those who have had for part of their lives someone to share the joys and duties and responsibilities, how often the sense of isolation, of being left out, can be real and devastating. Even those of us who have voluntarily chosen singleness know moments of loneliness when we feel as if we are all alone, with no one to share or encourage, with others seemingly a threat to us. Perhaps there have been moments when, like Elijah (v. 4), we feel like asking God that our lives may end.

God had a surprising message for Elijah—there were still 7000 who like him were loyal to God. For us too there is the message that not only does God love us, but there are many human friends who share our feelings and who need as we do to touch someone else in their loneliness. Be a search committee of one today to find someone who needs to be encouraged and heartened by your supportiveness.

 O God, our ever-present guide and friend, help me in my need to know that I am never really alone. Amen.

Think of a person who seems lonely and in need of encouragement. First pray for him or her, then call or send a greeting card to cheer the day.

■ GOD'S TIME AND PLACE

Esther 4:4-17: "Yet who knows—maybe it was for a time like this that you were made queen!" (v. 14).

This is the only story in the Bible, I believe, that credits God with placing a young woman in the competition to win a beauty contest. At any rate, that is how Mordecai seems to have assessed the situation, for out of Mordecai's home Esther had been taken to enter the competition for queenship (apparently no entrant in this competition complained about being treated solely as a sex object). Esther won. Later Mordecai came to Esther with the request that she try to save her people by a direct plea to a king who hadn't even acknowledged her existence for a whole month. Esther agreed, saying, "If I perish, I perish."

Not many of us are called on to take part in that kind of melodrama. But if we wish to keep our lives from becoming routine-bound and dull, we need Esther's willingness to engage in some meaningful adventure. The stakes may not be as high as in her case. But how about supporting an orphan in India? Or speaking your Christian convictions on a controversial neighborhood issue?

 Lord, when issues with high stakes come up in my life, I tend to pull back and disengage. Give me the courage to get involved in things that really matter. Amen.

Before the day is done, speak out on an issue where your Christian beliefs make a difference.

■ THE LONELINESS OF SUFFERING

Job 3:11-26: "Why is life given to a man whose way is hidden, whom God has hedged in?" (v. 23 NIV).

All of us, single or married, are alike in our need for companionship when things are going wrong for us. The Book of Job is an interesting study in the need for and the giving of comfort. So long as Job's friends sat quietly with him they were no doubt comforters indeed, but later, when they began to charge Job with unnamed sins and with being to blame for his own troubles, they would have done better to go home. Job is by their words pushed deeper into that sense of isolation and loneliness which is part of the problem of human suffering.

Both Satan and Job complained that God had hedged Job in (1:10 and 3:23). Satan said Job had never faced real spiritual choices—God had limited his options. Job saw himself hedged in by his suffering; he was left wanting to die.

To reach into the suffering of another person and help lift his or her loneliness by sharing it is a challenge to each of us. As singles, we need to be vigilant for those opportunities in the lives of other singles, willing to make ourselves available to meet each other's needs.

Give me a sensitivity, O Lord, to others and their feelings. May I be helpful in a healthy way that will reduce their loneliness. Amen.

Find a book or pamphlet which helped you in a time of discouragement. Send or take it to someone you know who is going through a time of suffering.

■ A REALISTIC PERSPECTIVE

Job 38:1-18: "Job, have you ever in all your life commanded a day to dawn?" (v. 12).

The Book of Job is often thought to deal with facing troubles with patience, but a more accurate assessment might be "keeping yourself in perspective." Job, growing more indignant with every day as his suffering continued and his "comforters" talked on, prepared an eloquent plea, a statement of his own integrity, which he would make if only he could get an audience before God. I would "hold my head high in his presence," he proclaims (31:37). But he never gets his chance. In question after question, God challenges Job to see himself in perspective, as creature rather than creator, dealing with one who brings rain even where no one lives (38:26) and commands a universe beyond earth. Job gets the point.

Because the traditional pattern of society is marriage, it is often more difficult for us who live as singles to keep ourselves in perspective. We are not—or are no longer—one half of a couple. We are individuals facing our unique situations, problems, and accomplishments. But we need to remember that there is much more to this life than our personal decisions and problems. We are each important, to God and to others, but our individual concerns are not the dominating aspect of human existence. Like Job, we need God's help to accept the reality that all of life does not center on us.

Lord, help me keep my perspective on life and on myself straight. Amen.

Take some extra prayer time to list items of greatest concern to you before God and ask him to show you in what order they belong.

■ A GOOD NIGHT'S REST

Psalm 4: "When I lie down, I go to sleep in peace; you alone, O Lord, keep me perfectly safe" (v. 8).

Isn't it amazing how many creakings and groanings a building can develop when you are lying in bed and cannot sleep, or how many problems which you seldom think of in the daytime demand solutions when you have lain sleepless for an hour? These fears may have nothing to do with things that "go boomp in the night," but they are very real to many who now live alone but who for years were accustomed to having someone else near them in the night—parents, spouse, or children now grown. An overactive imagination can turn every unexpected sound into a threat that chases all possibility of sleep.

David's life had countless times of real, not imaginary, danger. Saul's pursuit of him in his youth, responsibility for himself and his men in time of war, rebellion against him from within his own family—all of these could have caused him sleeplessness. Yet his confidence in God's care made him lie down and sleep. I find one of the best sedatives for sleeplessness is reviewing Bible passages, especially Psalm 23.

> The twilight shadows round me fall,
>   And night comes stealing on;
> But thou, dear Lord, art ever near,
>   My day when day is gone.
> Thy wings in love o'ershadow me,
>   The night with thee is light;
> I rest in thee, thou changeless One,
>   And wait the morning bright.
>
> (*Service Book and Hymnal* 233)

Keep your hymnal on your bedstand. If sleep is evasive, read the words of the evening hymns that it contains.

■ THE SACRAMENT OF THE MORNING

Psalm 5: "You hear my voice in the morning; at sunrise I offer my prayer and wait for your answer" (v. 3).

Not all singles live alone, but a great many do. Even those who live in small groups probably have their own morning routines as they prepare for work and the events of the day.

Our morning routine can be a morning sacrament. The one who keeps us from ever being completely alone waits for our "Good morning, Lord," and, as he has done every day of our lives before, offers us his grace. I can sip my cup of coffee and sit quietly knowing I love him—sometimes even knowing I feel angry with him—and be aware of his promises: "Lo, I am with you always," and "As your days, so shall your strength be." I can experience the deep quiet that can come in the early morning before the world's hustle begins. That stillness is worth getting up earlier for. It can be the sacrament of the morning, nourishing us and giving us strength for the day to come. Just as we meet him in the bread and wine at the altar, he will meet us in the coffee and toast of our morning routine.

Lord, make the beginnings of my days sacraments in which, through the daily elements of my life, you share your grace with me. I need it today and every day. Amen.

Take five minutes to sit quietly after your devotion and simply enjoy the quiet in your own heart. That stillness too can be a daily sacrament.

■ GOD'S DEFINITION OF MAN

Psalm 8: "Yet you made him inferior only to yourself; you crowned him with glory and honor" (v. 5).

The question of "What is man?" has absorbed the attention of many people through the centuries. The answers given have been vitally important in history. "Man is an economic being," said Karl Marx. "Man is primarily a sexual being," said Freud. "Man is a political being," said Machiavelli. "Man is a religious being," said the leaders of many religions. "There is one God and man is his creation," said the Bible writers. In each case, the definition shaped the definer's view and treatment of man.

Many of the answers given are not likely to leave us feeling very significant. We are seen to a great degree as appetites—one-sided appetites at that. We who are single may feel even less significant than those who are part of a family unit. How much more satisfying to be defined as "inferior only to God" and "crowned with glory and honor." To be a child of God is to be a significant creation. As we hear so often today, "God doesn't make junk." Don't forget when you wash your dishes to wear your crown.

 Lord, I thank you that you have loved me. Help me to learn to love myself with the right kind of love so that I will be free to love others rightly too. Amen.

On a card print the words, "I am God's workmanship. I am important to him." Tape the card on your bathroom mirror where you will see it the first thing every day.

■ OUR DEFINITION OF GOD

Ps. 18:1-19: "The Lord is my protector; he is my strong fortress. . . . He protects me like a shield; he defends me and keeps me safe" (v. 2).

We in New Testament times have in Jesus a revealing of what God is like. Old Testament writers over and over use metaphor—comparison to the familiar—to express their understanding of God. They call him *rock, shield, stronghold, shepherd* —always aware that there is more to him than their picture language can contain. They chose the metaphors their particular needs required.

David in Psalm 18 chose words to describe God that fit his own need for protection and refuge from his enemies. What descriptive words would we who live alone choose if we were to write a psalm about God and what he means to us? The ones others have used are meaningful to us too, but perhaps we would choose such expressions as *companion, loving presence, guide, comfort.* My personal Psalm 18 might read:

> I love thee, O Lord, my source of courage for
> the day.
> The Lord is my companion and my guide, my
> comfort in times of loneliness or hard decisions.
> He is the loving presence always near me,
> my source of wisdom in meeting life's demands.
> I call upon the Lord, who is worthy to be praised,
> and I need never feel deserted nor afraid.

Thank you, Lord God, that you have revealed yourself to us in the Bible and in the Living Word, Jesus. Amen.

Write a psalm, an expression of your own praise to God. If you need to, use a favorite psalm as a pattern.

■ A CONFIDENT FAITH

Ps. 18:31-50: "He makes my feet like the feet of a deer; he enables me to stand on the heights" (v. 33 NIV).

People who do not know the way of the believer sometimes look upon it as stilted, circumscribed with petty rules and regulations, hedged with negatives—a way of life for timid little ladies with cups of tea and embroidery hoops. The psalmist, whose images radiate confidence, has quite another outlook, an exuberance and zest for meeting even the battles of life. God keeps his lamp burning. With God he can conquer enemies and scale a wall. His feet, like those of a deer, carry him to the heights and, set on high places, do not slip.

The God we worship is not a God of petty limitations, one who narrows and limits our lives in dullness. In our living alone, he is not busy closing doors and windows upon us. The narrownesses we experience we bring upon ourselves by our hesitation to walk in paths that lead to where his work is done. If we allow him to lighten our darkness, he will show us the things he has for us to do, and as we follow with faith and joy we will be able to exult as David did: "With my God I can scale a wall."

 Lord, give me eyes to see the excitement there is in being teamed with the God of the multiverse in fulfilling his plans. Amen.

Put away something dull in color in your home and replace it with something bright as a reminder that God is not a drab presence in our lives.

■ THE UNSEEN FAULT

Psalm 19: "No one can see his own errors; deliver me, Lord, from hidden faults!" (v.12).

One of the advantages of living in a family circle, or at least in a circle of people who are close enough to be honest with each other, is that habits, mannerisms, or faults we develop can be made known to us by the comments or reactions of the group. It is difficult to be perceptive about our own lives if we do not have available the corrective of someone else's response to us. As singles, we need to be aware of the possibility that undesirable characteristics may develop in our personalities without our perceiving them. The psalmist is aware of this: faults and errors he may not be aware of may have crept into his life. He prays that the Lord may turn the light of his law on his actions and illuminate the hidden faults.

As singles we may be supportive friends to each other in this respect, helping each other to see ourselves honestly, not through veils hung over our faces by our self-love. Such correction, of course, needs to be given only when the receiver is open to it, and it must always be given with megadoses of tact and love.

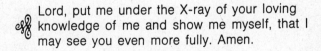 Lord, put me under the X-ray of your loving knowledge of me and show me myself, that I may see you even more fully. Amen.

Take a moment to examine your life. Have you developed any new habits of which you are unaware? Are they worth keeping?

■ THE FRIENDSHIP OF THE LORD

Psalm 25:1-15: "The Lord is the friend of those who obey him and he affirms his covenant with them" (v. 14).

One of the great privileges of life is to have a friend, a much richer thing than to have many acquaintances. In his book *A Nation of Strangers,* Vance Packard reports that a large percentage of Americans, mobile as we are, cannot name even a few people to whom they are close enough to turn with confidence when they really need someone. Friendship is a resource that needs constant nourishment and renewal. We who are singles know the importance of close friendships. For us they often take the place of family. We can express our joys, pour out our problems, share our interests and responses to life with real friends, just as we gladly are the listeners as they share their experiences with us.

Human friendships are precious. But even more precious is the friendship of the Lord. It too has a sharing. "He affirms his covenant with them." It too needs to be cherished and fed, in prayer and the study of his Word. This friendship—unlike the human friendships that sometimes fail us—will grow and develop all through this life, and find its fullest fruition in the life to come.

Prayer Suggestions: 1. Thank God for the opportunity for friendship with him.
2. Ask God for a blessing this day for your close friends, and pray that he will help you to be a worthy friend in return.

Seek out someone today who seems to be lacking in friends and show yourself a friend in his or her need.

■ THE UNSEEN INHABITANT

Psalm 27: "The Lord protects me from all danger; I will never be afraid" (v. 1).

After growing up in a family, it takes a while before we feel at ease in assuming some of the activities natural to those who live alone. Widows have told me how hard it is to go to church alone after years of going with their husbands. Others never get over a hesitation about coming home at night to an empty house or apartment. Some of the concern, no doubt, is for safety. I came home one night to my locked house to find a disordered bathroom—it definitely was not as I had left it. It took me a few minutes to realize that my student roomer who had told me he would be leaving town for the weekend must have changed his mind. I can smile at the episode now, but I didn't rest easily till I had searched the house and found that what I had assumed was true.

As believers, we never really come home to an empty house. Around us, before us, and behind us is the presence of one who has promised he will be with us always, surrounding us with love and concern. As we unlock the door and step inside, it is time to say, "Thank you, Lord, for being here when I come home."

Lord, in the moments of my life when I am a bit of a coward, please be my confidence. Amen.

Do you know people who stay home from events they would enjoy rather than go and come home alone? Invite one of them to go with you to an event you too would like to attend.

■ FACING THE FUTURE

Ps. 34:1-14: "The oppressed look to him and are glad; they will never be disappointed" (v. 5).

W hat a tremendous lift God provided for the psalmist when he freed him from all his fears! Fear is a natural emotion for a human being—"I, a stranger and afraid, in a world I never made" (A. E. Housman). The past has had its fears; the present has them; and, oh, the future, how full of them it sometimes seems! Those of us who live alone may have more fears for the future than do those who live in families. Fears for our safety, for what will happen to our health, for inflation, for old age: how often we resolutely turn our thoughts away from these things.

It is reassuring that we live in a time when society is more ready to help and care for us in emergencies than it has been in the past. The agencies we have supported with our taxes may, if other support systems fail, return that care to us in our need. But knowing that has less comfort for us than does the confidence we have in one who can make us radiant because we have tasted and seen that he is good. In the midst of every fear-arousing situation we can know by faith that God's strong arms surround us.

 When I look at my fears, O Lord, help me always to see them against the backdrop of your power and your love for me. Amen.

Take a minute to remember and smile at some specific times in your life when fears that sapped so much of your joy and energy turned out to be completely needless. Keep those times handy for use as ammunition when new fears arise.

■ THE FEAR OF THE YEARS

Ps. 37:23-31: "I am an old man now; I have lived a long time, but I have never seen a good man abandoned by the Lord or his children begging for food" (v. 25).

We live in a society that practically worships youth. Organizations and businesses thrive on our desire to look young and feel young. Cosmetics, clothing styles, plastic surgery—all get into the act of making us look young when we no longer are. With less back-breaking labor, both men and women look years younger than their parents did at the same age.

But looking young is not enough to keep people from fearing to grow older. With youth so admired, old age becomes a time to dread rather than a time to enjoy the wisdom and poise of a life well spent. The passing years can be more than usually traumatic for us who live alone and often worry about what problems a possible illness or immobility might bring.

The psalmist in our text is old; he has lived a long and observant life. He can state with assurance that God does not desert his people as the years go by—he is sufficient to their needs. That assurance can be ours as well.

Lord, keep us from spending our energies on our fears. Give us the trust to rest in the everlasting arms that are around us. Amen.

Take a few moments for a character study of a person from your acquaintance who has aged gracefully. What has been his or her secret? Is it one you are putting to use?

■ ONLY A PASSING GUEST

Ps. 39:4-13: "Like all my ancestors I am only your guest for a little while" (v. 12).

This psalm and the 90th Psalm stress what we all theoretically know but what becomes clearer as the years go by: our lives are briefer than we think. "Our life . . . fades away like a whisper" (90:9).

One can respond to that reality in various ways. We can sit back and say life is too brief to achieve our goals. Or we can determine to use the days to the full as they slip past us. How much more productive the second response! The skill I might have developed, the trip so yearned for, the project which might have benefited my neighborhood, the time spent with elderly relatives—these will never exist if my attitude is always to put them off till later.

God intends our lives to be full and interesting. He has provided dozens of options for our enjoyment, none of which may be claimed if we are ruled by our timidities. As singles, we must dare to seize the opportunities that exist for us; to reach out for what is there of joy and adventure. Letting our hesitancies shut down our options is not God's best for us.

 Lord, help me not to be ruled by my timidities but instead by a joyous confidence in your goodness. Amen.

What is one of the dreams you have so far put off for the future? Take some specific step today to get information on how you can bring it to pass without further delay.

◼ WHEN FRIENDS DESERT US

Psalm 41: "Even my best friend . . . has turned against me" (v. 9).

Whether we realize it or not, friends are terribly important to us. For those who are single, friends serve in many of the roles otherwise enacted by the immediate family. We count on their loyalty and love remaining constant as the years go on. Yet we are fortunate indeed if we have never known the experience of the poet who finds that a close friend has turned against him. He expected no support from his enemies, but the non-faithfulness of a friend is an even more cruel blow.

The times we need our friends most may be the times we are most likely to act in a way that turns them off. In like manner, the times our friends need us most may be the times they act in ways we disapprove.

The greatness of God's friendship for us is that it is dependable even when we are most unlovable. If we are to love others as he loves us, that means we express God's love to our friend even when he is most unlovely. That is not easy, but it is the Christ-like thing to do.

 Heavenly Father, help me to show my friends who depend on me the kind of friendship you have shown to me throughout my life. Amen.

Make a particular effort today to show your steadfast love to a friend on whose recent actions you have been inclined to frown.

■ ENJOYING GOD'S ARTWORK

Psalm 104: "Lord, you have made so many things! How wisely you made them all!" (v. 24).

Some activities are best done with a companion. But others are just as enjoyable if we do them alone. The intense observation of nature demonstrated in this psalm points to a sphere of activity we can richly enjoy all by ourselves. The grace of a swallow's flight, the miracle of engineering that is the spider's web, the mischief in the flicking of a squirrel's tail, the eagerness in a puppy's eyes: these are but a few of the myriad details of nature around us which show the variety, the complexity, and the wonder of God's world. Many of us see only a few of them. Some might just as well be blind. One can have 20/20 vision but see less than many who are physically blind.

In Bunyan's *Pilgrim's Progress* there is a muckraker who stands bent over, raking together the debris on the floor around him, never realizing that if he would stand erect his head would fit into a golden crown that hangs above him. If he had "eyes to see" he could find marvelous wonders in the world around him. So can we.

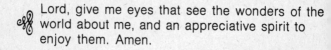

Lord, give me eyes that see the wonders of the world about me, and an appreciative spirit to enjoy them. Amen.

Stop right where you are to count 10 things in sight that have something beautiful about them. Keep noticing all day. Incidentally, when did you last read *Pilgrim's Progress*? It's worth another reading.

■ THE DEATH OF HIS SAINTS

Psalm 116: "Precious in the sight of the Lord is the death of his saints" (v. 15 NIV).

Also "precious in the sight of the Lord" is the *life* of his saints. That is easier to accept, isn't it, for us life-loving human beings? The preciousness of death is beyond our usual comprehension. Death in our culture is feared and hidden. The Hebrews found comfort in the face of death in having descendants to carry on the family identity and inheritance. He lives on in the hearts of others, in what he has done, in the lives of his children—all these we say in the face of death.

That consolation does not mean as much to a single person or to childless couples with no descendants to bear a family name into the future. We are driven back to the fact that to the Lord we are precious not for our descendants or our ancestors, but simply for ourselves. We are precious to him not for what we do but for who we are—his children. We are precious to him not only in our lives but in our death. We haven't been given the particulars of what happens in and after our death, but Jesus has told us "In my father's house are many rooms; . . . I go to prepare a place for you."

 Lord, make my attitudes toward both life and death healthy outgrowths of my faith in you. Amen.

Develop with a close friend the ability to talk as naturally about death as you do about other future events.

■ DEEPER IN THE WORD

Ps. 119:1-19: "Open my eyes, so that I may see the wonderful truths in your law" (v. 18).

As I choose activities I have time to do because I live alone, one of the most rewarding is systematic Bible study—not the few verses at a time of a devotional book but the study of a whole book from the Bible or a topical study. We would never read another book in as random a fashion as we do the Bible—a story here, a poem there, hardly ever a whole book at a time. Each book has a purpose not always identifiable from reading just snatches.

Unless you have done much Bible study on your own, you will fare better with the New Testament first—a gospel such as Mark, or a letter to early believers. Bible study helps are likely waiting in your church library or available from your church publishing house. Bible correspondence courses offered by various groups provide expert background to make the Bible meaningful.

A few hours a week of such study can deepen our spiritual roots. Our eyes will be opened, and we will truly see "wonderful truths in your law."

Holy Spirit, do your work in me by revealing Jesus to me in my study of your Word. Amen.

Set aside time today to read a complete book of the Bible—e.g., Philippians. Watch for what is revealed of Paul's purpose in writing to the church at Philippi— and to us.

■ MAKE YOUR PATH KNOWN

Ps. 139:1-12: "You see me, whether I am working or resting; you know all my actions" (v. 3).

This psalm makes it beautifully evident that our efforts to hide from God are futile. When we speak wistfully about "getting away from it all" we know better than to suppose that means getting away from God—and who would want to?

Just as it is comforting to know that God always knows our whereabouts, it is practical for those of us who live alone to let some other person know where we are if we will be unreachable for any length of time. This is not only a matter of safety, but also of convenience. Many of us have experienced the need to pass on a message of an emergency nature to someone who has left town with no word about his or her destination. Or we have gone off for a long weekend only to realize on the way that no one knows where we are or how to reach us. I expect too much of my friends if I expect them to "know all my actions" as God does. Having left word for them about my ways, I can still get away from it all in the company of my omnipresent Lord.

Lord, I am grateful for the constancy of your presence with me. Help me to be responsible in my actions so that others are not inconvenienced by them. Amen.

Arrange a mutual agreement with two close friends whereby each of you is kept aware of long-term absences of the others.

■ ALONE, BUT WELL KNOWN

Psalm 139: "Lord, . . . you know me. You know everything I do" (vv. 1, 2).

A result of people's living together in a family group is that the individual comes to be known, to be predictable, aware that facades are useless because people know him or her too well for a false front to work. Those of us who live as singles, however, often live without that intimate familiarity and can come to believe "Nobody really knows me."

Robert Frost in his poem "Revelation" speaks of people who hide behind words that "tease and flout, but oh, the agitated heart till someone really finds us out." Even God, he adds, yielded to the desire to make himself known. Have you noticed how often a small child playing hide-and-seek fears being hidden too long and must call out?

We can be of service to our friends by taking the time and effort to know them well, to be good listeners, to be understanding rather than judgmental. For ourselves, when tempted to feel that no one really understands us, we can remember the assurances of God's intimate knowledge of us. "You know everything I do" tells me I need never fear being unknown or misunderstood by him.

 Father, sometimes I find your knowledge of me frightening rather than comforting, but today I rejoice that you know me through and through. Amen.

Think over your associations with others. Is there someone with whom you put on a facade? Watch for ways to make that relationship more sincere.

■ THE TROUBLEMAKER

Prov. 6:12-22: "There are seven things that the Lord hates and cannot tolerate: . . . one is a man who stirs up trouble among friends" (vv. 16, 19).

People who live as singles have no corner on gossip, but we often do have problems that are caused by people who seek attention by tale-bearing and telling falsehoods about others. Verses 12-14 give an almost humorous picture of such a person, winking and pointing his finger at others. But the results of such a person's activity are far from humorous. Friendships— and we all need our friendships—are destroyed, suspicion is aroused, opportunities are lost, all for the sick satisfaction of someone whose speech is seasoned with jealousy and a desire to cause trouble rather than with love.

Knowing how to handle these people in our circle of acquaintances or friends is a problem. They too need friendships and a place in the sun; they too are loved by God. Yet we cannot let ourselves become a part of the slander they peddle. Frank but firm refusal to share in their stirring of trouble, along with silence about them and their tales, may be our best method of reducing the damage done. Sometimes an evil account may even be laughed into disrepute.

 Gracious Father, make me sensitive to the ways I myself may stir up trouble without realizing it. Amen.

Check back to our Scripture reading to see which of the other things God hates may have any relevance to your own life.

■ THE LIBERAL SPIRIT

Prov. 11:19-31: "Some people spend their money freely and still grow richer. Others are cautious, and yet grow poorer" (v. 24).

W hen the psalmist describes the righteous who are not forsaken in old age, he says, "At all times he gives freely and lends to others" (Ps. 37:26). While we need to avoid the rigid ancient expectation that the righteous are always prosperous and the wicked necessarily poor, we find in our text a principle that we can see again and again demonstrated: "Be generous and you will be prosperous. Help others, and you will be helped" (11:25).

What does this mean to those of us who live alone and are responsible for our own economic needs? Can we afford to have a liberal heart? What of the future? Will we have enough?

The liberal person described above had, we can be sure, two characteristics: a big heart for the needs of others, and a certainty in his soul that God will never be in debt to anyone. What is given to God will be repaid manyfold. So we can afford to give first of ourselves to those we can aid, and second, to give of our means without fear that our giving will impoverish us. God, we are told, loves a cheerful giver.

 Thank you, gracious Father, for all you have given me. Help me have faith enough not to withhold what I should give. Amen.

Plan right now a specific way to give at least 15 minutes of yourself today to someone who needs you.

■ THE PRIVACY OF SINGLENESS

Prov. 14:1-26: "Your joy is your own; your bitterness is your own. No one can share them with you" (v. 10).

M any of us who live alone did not plan it that way. A marriage did not work out, we lost a mate, a romance did not mature as expected. It would be interesting to see a study done on those who choose to live alone to see how many of us are such private people that we did not marry because we could not tolerate anyone's intrusion on our privacy. Mary Wilkins Freeman's perceptive story, "A New England Nun," portrays a woman whose betrothed returns after a long absence spent in making his fortune only to find that she cannot deal with his intrusion into her immaculate house and placid routine.

There is, of course, an inner place in our lives where none of us admit others, as the writer of Proverbs knew. In that inwardmost part of us are hidden away those hurts we could not tell even our best friend as well as the joys so deep we have no way to express them. We need to remember that there is one who knows us better than we know ourselves who can help us deal with the bitternesses and release the joys.

 I am grateful, O Lord, to be known fully by you. Help me to handle in a healthy way both my bitternesses and my joys. Amen.

We can do much good by sharing our joys. Share one of yours with someone who needs a lift today.

■ THE CHEERFUL DISPOSITION

Prov. 17:15-28: "Being cheerful keeps you healthy. It is slow death to be gloomy all the time" (v. 22).

W hen people are happy, they smile, . . . happy people always enjoy life," says the writer of Proverbs (15:13, 15). He knew a great deal about what we today call psychosomatic medicine. Doctors tell us of the numbers of hospital beds filled by people whose illnesses, while they are real, have their origins in the emotions and in negative mental attitudes.

If our living alone involves too much being alone, we can come to be among the many who suffer from depression. The more depressed we become, the more we withdraw into ourselves and avoid others. The more we withdraw, the more depressed we become.

Doctors and pastors can do much to help us when we are depressed. Prayer, reading our Bibles, and the companionship of understanding friends can also help. Exerting ourselves to get out of the house, to do something different—go to a concert, park, museum, or shopping mall—can help us get our attention off ourselves. There is a truth to the old saw, "God helps those who help themselves." We need never fear that his love and concern have deserted us.

 Lord, grant me the cheerful heart that does good like a medicine both to me and to others around me. Amen.

Plan within a week to do some relaxing and enjoyable activity designed simply to be refreshment for your spirit.

■ THE WRONG EXCUSE

Prov. 24:1-12: "You may say that it is none of
your business, but God knows and judges
your motives" (v. 12).

Living alone does not confer on us some sort of
freedom or absolution from responsibility toward
others. There are those who seem to assume that if
they can be free from needing anyone else's assistance,
they are thereby freed from any need to assist others.
Such an attitude probably has its roots in a complex
psychological history, but as followers of Christ we
can never shrug off another's need even if we claim
ignorance of it. There is an interdependence in all of
life that ties us inseparably to each other. Short of
being nosy and intrusive, it is our business to be aware
of the needs of others and to act as we are able in order
to meet them. What tragedies in human communities,
how many suicides, how many crimes, could have
been prevented if people who lived next door or in the
next apartment, who worked in the same office, who
worshiped in the same church, had accepted the fact
that we are none of us excused by glibly saying
"It was none of my business," when we should have
made it our business to know. That is a hard truth
to bear.

Lord, make me perceptive about the needs of
others and willing to help meet them. Keep me
also from blaming myself when there was no
possible way that I could know their particular
need. Amen.

**If someone lives near you whom you have never met,
seek an opportunity today to at least speak to him
or her.**

■ THE DAUGHTERS OF THE LEECH

Prov. 30:5-19: "Let me be neither rich nor poor
. . . give me only as much food as I need" (v. 8).

To find admirers of the butterfly, the moth, the chipmunk is fairly easy. Even the mosquito is accorded a place in the food chain. But the leech is seldom commended: it only takes, and its result is the weakening of the host. "A leech has two daughters, and both are named 'Give me!'" (v. 15).

With the stress on "things" that is so evident in our society, we need to actively resist attaching too great an importance to them, or else we may be dominated by them. There is sometimes a danger for a person who lives alone to replace human companionship with an attachment to possessions. It is natural to be fond of an item that is beautiful or has warm emotional associations. But wealth in possessions, for all its tangibleness, makes a poor object of love. Wealth in friendship and service is far better and more enduring.

Undeniably we need resources that keep us from the poverty level, things that meet our actual needs. But when our riches, our most valued possessions, are material things beyond our needs, we may need to look again lest our riches be shown false, and our treasures be those of earth instead of heaven.

Father, help me to possess my possessions rather than being possessed by them. Amen.

Many voices are calling on us in our affluent society to live more simply. Make at least one decision today that will fit with having only "as much food as I need."

■ A RIGHT TIME FOR EVERYTHING

Eccles. 3:1-15: "He has set the right time for everything. He has given us a desire to know the future, . . . " (v. 11).

The more I read these verses from Ecclesiastes, the more I marvel at the wisdom contained in them. How profound their relationship to ethics! So often an act that is desirable at one time is obviously wrong at another. Or what is destructive in one period turns out to fit a real need in another.

During our lives we are all faced with the need to make decisions. The responsibility for these decisions has a challenge and stimulation for us: it feels great to find one has done the right thing. But these decisions can also be a worrisome burden under which we struggle. Would I do better to change jobs? Would another type of housing be better for me? Am I investing my savings profitably?

Even if we are single, these decisions need not be ours alone. Our pastor or banker or a trusted relative may give us much good assistance. And God, who "has set the right time for everything," will help us to know when the time and the act are right if we seek his counsel.

 Thank you, Lord, for making everything beautiful in its time. Help me to know one time from another. Amen.

Which of the times in this selection from Ecclesiastes has a special relevance for your life today? Offer your decision concerning that time to God for guidance.

THE HEALTHINESS OF FLEXIBILITY

Eccles. 7:1-14: "When things are going well for you, be glad, and when trouble comes, just remember: God sends both happiness and trouble" (v. 14).

The author of Ecclesiastes, it is evident, never read a book or took a course on the power of positive thinking. We can tell that from the early verses of our chapter. Many Hebrews opposed the inclusion of this book in the canon of the Bible, but its supporters finally won out.

Among the proverbs are some wise sayings, however, such as the verse above. It emphasizes the need for flexibility in meeting the circumstances of life, a quality those of us who live alone and handle our own affairs must develop. A resiliency, the ability to bounce with the blows and not to despair when events go against us, is something we need. The person who cannot adapt to the adversities of life will find it hard to be independent and able to live life at a stable pace.

The God who made life a composite of joy and adversity is able both to heighten our joy and to keep us on an even keel in adversity. If we allow him to do them both, we will not need to conclude that death is better than life. Nor need we believe that "it is all useless . . . like chasing the wind" (2:26).

 Lord, like everyone else I need to be able to adapt to both joy and adversity. Help me to accept both as from you. Amen.

Take time to meditate on the past year. Find a reason to thank God for a specific adversity which by now you can understand came to you from his love.

■ KNOWING WHO WE ARE

Isa. 43:1-11: "I have called you by name—
you are mine" (v. 1).

To be accepted by others is very important to all
of us. Our sense of identity is formed to a great
extent by those who say of us, "You are mine." This
has been particularly true for women down through
history—they have been assigned their places by their
relationships with men. They were someone's
daughter, sister, or wife, and named accordingly.

The Hebrews through the history narrated by their
Scriptures were named by their identity—they were
called the people of God. Everyone who was called by
his name was to come to him. That includes us too. In
a special way, the word *Christian* names us as people.
Too often the word is used loosely only to refer to
any individual in a "Christian" country, or even
to one side in a war.

Those of us who live alone need a strong sense of
our identity to recognize our worth as individuals.
Christ says to us as we seek to follow his way, "I have
called you by name—you are mine." We bear his name,
and by it we know who we are, and whose we are.

O Lord, as you have named me as yours, I
would name you as mine, and thank you that I
may have this relationship with you. Amen.

List for yourself five ways in which your life will be
different today because God assures you that you bear
his name and belong to him.

■ ENGRAVED ON GOD'S HANDS

Isa. 49:8-18: "Even if a mother should forget her child, I will never forget you. . . . I have written your name on the palms of my hands" (vv. 15-16).

Have you ever been afflicted by the sort of person to whom you can be introduced over and over without his ever remembering that he has met you before? Surely few things can leave a person feeling more flat and faceless—we feel we have made no impression at all. (Probably the real truth is that the offender has a poor memory.)

What a wondrous comfort to know that those whom God has met in the grace of baptism he never forgets! In that act our names are written on the palms of his hands as his children; we are established more certainly in his memory than is a child in the memory of a mother.

Those of us who live as singles treasure that unfailing memory of the God who has made us his own. If human friends and associates forget our birthdays, forget their appointments with us, and leave us feeling faceless, we can be confident that the one who has our names in the palms of his hands has not forgotten us. And we ourselves must be mindful of letting our friends know that in our consciousness they live and are dear to us.

 Prayer Suggestion: Name before God occasions or decisions soon coming in your life when you will especially need to know that he has not forgotten you.

Check your memory or your files and send a card to someone you would otherwise have left ungreeted for an important occasion in his or her life.

■ STILL IN PROCESS

Isa. 64:1-9: "We are like clay, and you are like the potter. You created us" (v. 8).

Have you ever watched a potter at work? How skillful the hands that shape the vessel! But there are times when she recognizes that something is wrong, and she peels the clay off the form and begins again. One can never be sure what the vessel will look like until it is finished—the touch of the artist can make changes as long as it is in process.

It may look for us as we live our lives as singles that we have become what we are by our own decision and effort. If we are believers, there is another explanation: the divine potter is at work, constantly molding and reshaping according to the pliability of the human clay. We are not finished yet; we are still in process.

Discouragement over our own progress is easy. We see others who are so much more attractive or sparkling or mature or intelligent. Don't be discouraged. You are not finished yet. You are still in process. When the process is complete, you will be like Christ, for the Spirit will have shaped you after the model he provides.

Great divine potter, make me responsive to your molding of my life. Amen.

Identify one of the aspects of your life that still needs more work by the potter. What help can you give him?

■ THE SINGLENESS OF JEREMIAH

Jer. 16:1-5, 19-21: "Do not marry or have children in a place like this" (v. 2).

The person who would fully follow Paul's advice that "each one should go on living according to the Lord's gift to him" (1 Cor. 7:17) may find him- or herself called to be single. God may have a special work planned that he or she could do best when practicing the gift of singleness. So it was with Jeremiah. Called by God to be his prophet, to bring his message to his people, Jeremiah is told to remain single. And God knows best. The persecution and stress of Jeremiah's career would hardly have led to satisfactory married life.

Paul, too, saw his singleness as a gift to be used for God's purposes. He could have, like Peter, had a wife to travel about with him, but single he could give his entire energies to his mission.

Our Lord also remained single. He showed a great kindness to and concern for women, but his ministry was one in which he was committed eminently to his Father's plan.

The gift of singleness is one that can be offered to our Lord to be used for his purposes. Then it will be truly a blessing.

Lord God, if there is something in your kingdom that needs doing that can best be done by me as a single, give me the opportunity and the willingness to help. Amen.

Think through the activities of your church to see if there is something you as a single person might best be able to do.

■ HALLOWED BE THY NAME

Ezek. 36:16-38: "That made me concerned for my holy name" (v. 21).

To each his or her own name is important. Our names are a symbol, a representation of us in the eyes of others. If someone treats our name with disrespect, it becomes an attack on us personally.

It is obvious in our society that a great many people give little respect to the name of God. But God does. Not only the use of his name but obedience to his commands is involved in his concern for his holy name. In their disobedience his people had become careless in giving honor to his name.

As one who lives alone, I can keep my home from being a place where God's name is treated lightly. Few of us can control our work environment so adequately. Unfortunately, one of the changes in contemporary society is that the presence of women no longer safeguards against the profaning of God's name. Many of them join in its abuse.

"You shall not take the name of the Lord your God in vain" is still one of the Ten Commandments. Christians still pray, "Hallowed be thy name." In the midst of much profanation, we can keep our homes and our persons places where God's name is honored.

 Prayer Suggestion: In your prayer, meditate on the meaning of "Hallowed be thy name" and what that petition commits us to in our daily lives.

Examine with a friend ways in which you can handle offensive use of God's name that will leave a positive witness. In what sorts of situations is it best to say nothing?

■ DANIEL'S DIET

Dan. 1:1-16: "So from then on the guard let them continue to eat vegetables instead of what the king provided" (v. 16).

The author of Daniel sounds like a modern nutritionist—natural foods and lots of vegetables. Daniel and his friends saw in their eating habits an expression of a way of life related to their religious faith. They fared well.

Proper nutrition is a problem for many who live alone. Somehow it is not very interesting to prepare food for just one. Nutritionally healthful food seems to take more effort than it is worth for just one person, or so we say. So we fix another sandwich, we overload with starches. It is hard to shop for only one, so we buy snacks.

Our nutrition, like that of Daniel, is a part of a life-style pleasing to God. It affects our health and our energies, as many of us learn from sad experience. We can use a meal as a chance for fellowship with our friends; cooking can be more interesting if we do it for someone else and they for us. We live in a society in which much of our contact with others happens around food. It is important that we know how to choose our food in a way that promotes our health as well as our sense of good fellowship.

Lord, make me concerned about proper food for mind, soul, and body. Amen.

Plan a treat in your food preparation that is nutritionally desirable even if it takes a bit of extra work.

■ A SAVING SENSE OF HUMOR

Jonah 1:15-17; 2:10: "Then the Lord ordered the fish to spit Jonah up on the beach, and it did" (2:10).

Some would find it irreverent to ascribe a sense of humor to a biblical writer. I do not. In fact, it seems to me the God responsible for the impudence of the squirrel and the appearance of the armadillo obviously has a good sense of humor. So did the writer of the book of Jonah. On the other hand, Jonah, as his story develops, shows a lack of one. Perhaps it is expecting too much to think he should have showed one. Do you suppose the writer believed his subject would ever come to a point from which he could look back at this experience and chuckle over the predicament of the big fish who finally had to disgorge the undigestible object he had swallowed? Or smile at a vision of himself as he scrambled free of the seaweed and fishy entrails?

Keeping a sense of humor about our misfortunes is vitally important to those of us who live as singles. If we lose our ability to find the humorous aspects of our misfortunes, we lose a part of our ability to see events in perspective. Once in a while, at least, we need to see our Jonah experiences from the perspective of the fish.

Lord, keep me able, please, to see the humor in the predicaments I find myself facing. Amen.

Terence Fretheim has written a delightful study of the book of Jonah (*The Message of Jonah*, Augsburg). Make sure your church library has a copy, and read it for yourself.

■ THE POUTING PROPHET

Jonah 3:1—4:3: "He changed his mind and did not punish them as he had said he would. Jonah was very unhappy about this and became angry" (3:10; 4:1).

Jonah is a difficult person to like, though it is easy to sympathize with him. None of us likes to lose face by having our prophecies turn out wrong. This happened to Jonah, and he was greatly offended. It is hard to imagine prophets like Isaiah or Jeremiah anything but joyful if their proclamations of judgment had been followed by repentance and the averting of doom. But not Jonah. "God, I knew you were like that, so permissive I would only lose face by proclaiming what you said."

As singles we may feel this way too, when our decisions at times expose us to losing face. It is a mark of maturity to have things obviously go against what we have tried to achieve and still be able to respond gracefully with no Jonah-like sulking.

Lord, I pray that you will develop in me the kind of disposition that can bounce back with grace from disappointment and the kind of faith that trusts you to show me something better. Amen.

If in recent days someone has had to put up with pouting on your part, make today the time for a good-natured apology.

■ THE DANGERS OF SELF-PITY

Jonah 4: "He made a shelter for himself and sat in its shade, waiting to see what would happen to Nineveh" (v. 5).

One of the temptations we face as human beings—and possibly even more often as singles—is self-pity, one of the least attractive tendencies in our nature. It is so easy when troubles or embarrassments or failures plague us to draw within ourselves, bar the doors, and settle down to feel sorry for ourselves. To be told that others are in worse predicaments than ours is no help; we have decided to indulge in the cancerous luxury of self-pity. Just as cancer cells proliferate, so our self-pity feeds on everything adverse that happens. So it was with Jonah.

The book of Jonah is full of God's appointments for the education of Jonah. There is a great storm (1:4) to stop him in his flight; a large fish (1:17) to give him safety and thinking time; a successful message to proclaim (3:2) to make the effort worthwhile; a plant to give him shade (4:6), a worm (4:7) and a hot east wind (4:8) to compel him to listen to God's assessment of his behavior. But there is no happy ending for Jonah, no sign he gave up his self-pity. Barnaclelike, it clung to him, as it will to us. There is a time to be gentle and understanding with ourselves, but self-pity should be dealt with firmly lest it possess us.

Father, keep me from the trap of self-pity, especially about these matters which I name before you in my heart: _____, _____, _____. Amen.

Put on the frame of your door where you can see it as you leave your home a card on which you have printed the words: Today I will refuse to yield to self-pity.

■ A PEOPLE OF PEACE

Mic. 4:1-7: "They will hammer their swords into plows . . ." (v. 3).

Singles are sometimes thought not to have as much at stake in war as do the married, but single men are more often directly involved as soldiers—no family deferments for them. Single women predominate in auxiliary units. Singles are free to move to work in defense plants or to go as nurses in military units. As singles we have just as much reason to yearn for a day when swords shall be hammered into plows and spears into pruning knives.

It is amazing and horrifying when we look at history to see how often churches have not only kept silent in the face of the approach of war but even encouraged and made use of war for their own political purposes. From what we can learn about the early Christian era, Christians of that time did not bear arms, but once the faith became official and governments became Christian, things changed.

Singles, along with others knowledgeable about the terrible risks to human existence implicit in modern warfare, have a responsibility to exert influence on those who rule to settle disagreements by peaceful means, to reject greed as a guide to national policy, to be people of peace rather than of strife.

Lord, make me an instrument of your peace. Amen.

Read at least two articles or editorials dealing with national problems or concerns. Develop a habit of looking at such issues from all sides before making up your mind about them.

■ THE RULER OF THE STORM

Nah. 1:3-8: "Where the Lord walks, storms arise; the clouds are the dust raised by his feet" (v. 3).

Even many of us who live alone quite contentedly appreciate human companionship when a storm strikes. Even those who find in the brilliance of lightning and the majesty of thunder a thrill and an excitement would just as soon have some company. Those who are afraid of wind and storm cower in their own special safe places. It is easy to see why our ancestors worshiped the powers of nature which they understood little and feared much.

The Hebrews, unlike many of their neighbors, did not worship the forces of nature. They saw their God as the force behind nature, responsible for its creation and preservation, and ruling its forces. They also believed, as we are less likely to do today, that his direction of nature was his judgment on evil.

Storms can be a reminder for us of the power of the God we worship. It is sensible to take such precautions as we can. Beyond that, what is there to do but remember that the God of the storm has made himself known to us as the God of love in Christ Jesus? Even if we are injured, that does not mean we are separated from his love.

Great God of storm and power, thank you that nothing can snatch me out of your hands. Amen.

Check the safety factors in the place where you live. Determine the safest spot to be during a storm in your area, then don't worry about it further.

■ THE RESPONSIBILITY OF AN INVESTOR

Mal. 3:1-12: "Bring the full amount of your tithes to the temple, . . ." (v. 10).

People who live alone do not necessarily have fewer demands on their finances than others. Some help younger relatives go on to school. Others have barely enough income to meet their own needs. Some have debts. But many of us who live alone do have financial independence, and can decide for ourselves what we will share with our church and other good causes.

God's basic command about giving began in the Old Testament with the tithe. Offerings were in addition to the tithe. We hear less about the tithe in the New Testament, but proportionate giving, "as God has prospered you," is encouraged.

Single Christians in most churches can play an important part by sharing their income. We should take this responsibility seriously. Do we give all our gifts to our congregation or share with other religious and community causes too? Does our church suffer if we give instead to more sensational and visible pleas from the electronic church? God expects us to use wisely that which he has given to us. Not all good causes bear equal fruit. We need to look for fruit and be wise investors in the kingdom.

Lord, I thank you for the material gifts I have received from you. Guide me in my use of what belongs to you. Amen.

Take a look today at the record of your giving to church and benevolence in the past two years. Does a careful examination show that you could invest kingdom money more wisely?

■ HE KNOWS FROM EXPERIENCE

Matt. 4:1-11: "After spending forty days and nights without food, Jesus was hungry" (v. 2).

I cannot even imagine what it would be like to be all alone, except for satanic forces, for forty days. That Jesus could endure it is a testimony to his faith and obedience. When I make resolutions about what I will accomplish during vacation, I imagine my efficient use of all that time I will have alone. None of this constant dependence on others! But I find I do well if I make it through the second day without an urgent need to see a friend, or at least to talk with one.

We cannot know the depths of loneliness that Christ experienced on our behalf. Not only the forty days and nights, but the separation from the Father and heaven, the isolation from God in the Calvary experience, the utter failure of his friends to give comfort in Gethsemane. But we can know in our own attacks of loneliness that he has experienced and can share our feelings.

I could never really sympathize with someone who was homesick until I had an attack myself far from home and in a new job. Jesus had an even deeper experience of loneliness. He knows how to sympathize with and strengthen us through bleak days.

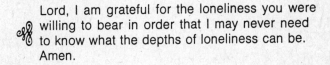

Lord, I am grateful for the loneliness you were willing to bear in order that I may never need to know what the depths of loneliness can be. Amen.

Plan ahead for a special treat on a day when loneliness threatens to turn into a problem.

■ NONVIOLENCE, JESUS FASHION

Matt. 5:38-48: "If anyone slaps you on the right cheek, let him slap your left cheek too" (v. 39).

When I teach the Sermon on the Mount in my course on the Bible as literature, a frequent response to verse 39 is, "But of course he didn't really mean that." My students are responding just as most people have ever since Jesus' days on earth. But the evidence in the Gospels is that Jesus *did* mean just what he said. There is no greater example of turning the other cheek than Jesus abused by the soldiers of Pilate. The church as a whole and individual believers all need to compare Jesus' words and his actions before they throw aside what he said.

Our society has lost much of its suspicion and hostility toward singleness as a life-style. But each of us will find occasion to react to attitudes and words that rouse anger and resentment in us. We must decide if we will follow Jesus in his nonviolence—including the nonviolence of our speech as well as our acts. If we would be Christ-like we do not have the option of "telling someone off" for our own satisfaction, no matter how many psychological theories advocate that. We may need to speak the truth frankly, but not for the pleasure of getting revenge.

Lord, I find it so easy to hold anger and resentment toward others. Grant that I might show more of your spirit in my relationships with those against whom I would like just a little bit of revenge. Amen.

Go out of your way today to show love toward someone who rouses resentment or anger in you by word or act.

■ THE SPECK AND THE LOG

Matt. 7:1-14: "Why, then, do you look at the speck in your brother's eye and pay no attention to the log in your own eye?" (v. 3).

Translators trying to show the force of the contrast between a brother's fault and our own use a variety of words for speck and log: *mote* and *beam, sliver* and *plank.* Jesus is using hyperbole, a purposeful exaggeration. A log cannot fit into the human eye, but the point he is making is clear: I can be so obsessed with a trivial fault in someone else that I fail to see the obvious and serious flaw in myself.

Those of us who live as singles have so much of our own company that it is easy to become accustomed to our failures. "We are the way we are," we say. But for variety we may become very observant of others, and critical of them in the ways they differ from us. It may be over something as trivial as how often they do their dishes.

To give other people room to live their lives does not always come naturally to us. I find it does not to me. I can be full of frank suggestions as to what others should do (I call them frank; they likely say bold). I need to remember that, like me, they are still in process.

 Lord, help me to be more concerned with perfecting myself and less with improving others. Amen.

Think of an action on the part of a friend that really irritates you. Try to find out why you are so bothered by it and how you can reduce the importance you give it.

■ THE FOES OF ONE'S HOUSEHOLD

Matt. 10:29-39: "I did not come to bring peace, but a sword" (v. 34).

Those of us who are at peace with family and relatives may forget there are those who live as singles because "a man's worst enemies will be the members of his own family." This is a painful kind of singleness because it results from a brokenness of those relationships around which daily life usually centers. There are children who leave home to get away from tensions with parents, partners in marriage alone because there no longer is a oneness left, parents who are lonely because values differ between generations.

When the rifts occur over the presence or absence of a commitment to Christ, his words, "I did not come to bring peace, but a sword," are applicable. When a loved one would keep us from life in Christ, a sword severs the closeness of the relationship. If we interfere with someone else's obedience to faith, we are the sword-wielders.

The sword will be removed when love and prayer bear their fruit in the healing of relationships and memories. That takes time, and nagging will not help. Perhaps the healing will be fully evident only in the life after this. But the promises of God are dependable. There will be a time in which broken relationships will be made whole.

Lord, make me a healer of brokenness, not a wielder of swords. Amen.

Invite someone you know who is saddened by broken family relationships to have a meal with you this week.

■ THE DANGERS OF EMPTINESS

Matt. 12:43-50: "Then it goes out and brings along seven other spirits even worse than itself" v. 45).

Not to grow is to begin to die. In a similar sense, we may say that not to keep supplying something new to our spirits is to risk emptiness of spirit. Scientifically speaking, we know nature abhors a vacuum and tries in any way possible to fill it. An empty farmhouse or resort cottage seems to invite vandalism or robbery. In the story Jesus tells, an empty house, even though once cleansed, is an invitation to demonic possession.

Those of us who live as singles often find it easy, living without the unpredictability of events in the family grouping, to let life become routine-ridden, habit-dominated, till freshness and newness have been emptied out of our existence. It is worth breaking out of routine once in a while if for no other reason than to maintain some flexibility of personality and life. There are too many demons of envy, rigidity, and intolerance toward others and their ways which can fill the vacuum if we do not seek to maintain an openness to what is new and a flexibility in our encounters with those about us.

Lord, keep me mentally and emotionally alive and growing. Amen.

Plan an interesting way to vary your routine for the next week. Evaluate at the end of the week whether the change has something to offer.

■ TELLING IT LIKE IT IS

Matt. 13:1-12: "For the person who has something will be given more, so that he will have more than enough; but the person who has nothing will have taken away from him even the little he has" (v. 12).

Some of the sayings of Jesus set up ideals for us to strive for. Others are simply statements of how things really operate in life—and we can trust him to tell it like it is. His statement in verse 12 has taken me my lifetime to understand. It seems so unfair, so opposite to the way things should be if justice exists, yet how true it is to human existence. We see it in economic life: the one with plenty of capital is the one whose wealth increases. The one with too little to invest cannot enjoy high rates of interest, and the poor have no capital from which to earn interest at all. We see it in the intellectual world: the one with keen perception grasps easily and becomes learned. The one with low intelligence cannot hold on to even those few skills he struggles so hard to learn. We see the same thing socially: the already-popular single has hosts of admirers; the one with less attraction for others finds it difficult to gain any friends.

Jesus here was speaking of those who were receptive to the seed of his word. If we are receptive (and all we need to be is empty and willing), we can have the abundance Jesus promises. It will be ours not of our deserving but by his grace. Then to us who have received, even more will be given.

Lord, grant me abundant fruit from the seed of your word. Amen.

So often our study of the Word is by bits and pieces. Again today, find a short book and read it in its entirety, watching especially for the author's purpose.

◼ HANDLING DECISIONS

Matt. 21:28-32: " 'I don't want to,' he answered, but later he changed his mind and went" (v. 29).

The necessity to make both frequent small decisions and occasional big ones can be troublesome whether we live alone or with others, but many who live alone, especially if that is a recent condition, can find this need traumatic. Their energy and joy in the day are sapped by a fear of wrong decisions, by constant changes of position on decisions, by the tendency of trivial decisions long fussed over to seem major ones. Some are like the sons of our text, each of whom was indecisive.

Once we have learned the facts necessary for making a sensible decision, sought counsel when that is wise, prayed about the matter, and made a decision, we should step out in faith that the decision can be trusted and implemented unless new facts appear. A constant seesawing is seldom any help. If the answer is not clear, it may often be wise to postpone the decision if we can until we see the way more clearly, but once the decision is made we should hold to it unless there is real cause for change. We cannot always go limping from one side of a question to the other.

 Lord, please give me good common sense and then keep me from constantly vacillating in my decisions. Amen.

Take time today to develop a good list of questions to ask yourself about any important decision in your life—e.g., "Is this decision realistic in the light of my income?"

■ THE DANGER OF TIMIDITY

Matt. 25:14-30: " . . . so I went off and hid your money in the ground" (v. 25).

A danger for those of us who live alone is the natural tendency to become overly protective of what we have and defensive about what is expected of us. Since I have to manage my own affairs, I am not going to let myself get into a position that will create problems. There is no one to protect my interests but me, and I am not going to take on more than I can handle.

While those attitudes are natural and to a degree sensible, how similar they make us to the third servant in our text! He wasn't taking any risks either. He was taking care of Number One. But God did not approve of his caution and punishment followed.

Our God is the great risk-taker. He risked the best he had to bring us to himself. He risks being rejected every time he calls us closer to himself. He risks our misunderstanding every time he denies our good in order to give us his best. He asks that in sharing the love and the talents he has given us with others, we be risk-takers. Of course there will be times we will be hurt and rejected, but if we walk his way, the risks will be worth the results.

 My Father, thank you that you were willing to risk all that it took to bring me to yourself. Give me the wisdom to know when I should be a risk-taker. Amen.

Take the risk today of real friendliness toward someone from whom you fear a rebuff.

■ THE CHRIST IN OTHERS

Matt. 25:31-46: "Whenever you did this for one of
the least important of these brothers of mine,
you did it for me!" (v. 40).

M ost of us have no trouble understanding that when
we have accepted an office on a church board or
given money for missions or raised our pledge that
we have done these things as unto Jesus. We've heard
people say that those who live singly do not take
their share of community responsibility, and we
surely want to demonstrate that we are not like that
in our service in the church. People in our church may
not exactly fit the definition of the "least important
of these," but they are surely brothers, right?

Jesus has a way of saying things that complicates
the easy answer. The "least important of these" he
speaks of include the hungry and thirsty, strangers and
unclothed, diseased and imprisoned. What do we
have to do with such people? They may be unsanitary—
even dangerous. Isn't it enough if we give a little
more to the benevolence budget at church? Maybe
some of that filters through to these people.

But is that really doing it as unto Jesus? Doesn't that
require more personal involvement? I can't suppose
he is unclothed, diseased, imprisoned, can I? Most of
us need to give more attention to that question.

 Lord Jesus, give me the kind of spiritual vision
I need to see you in the least of these,
my brothers. Amen.

**Check your wardrobe and set aside something warm
and serviceable to help meet someone else's need.**

■ A LIVING SACRIFICE

Matt. 26:26-35: "Take and eat; this is my body. . . .
Drink from it, all of you. This is my blood. . . . "
(vv. 26, 27 NIV).

Jesus several times said to his disciples that as he
was, so they were to be in this world. In these verses
we find Jesus speaking of himself as broken bread
and poured-out wine, offered for their partaking,
their forgiveness, their nourishment—and not only
theirs but for all. If we are to be as he is in this world,
does that not mean that we too are to be "living
sacrifices, holy and pleasing to God—which is your
spiritual worship" (Rom. 12:1)? Since we serve God
in this life by our ministry to other people, can we
not say that we too are to be broken bread and
poured-out wine for the nourishment and refreshment
of others?

That kind of language is not very acceptable in
our day with its emphasis on self-fulfillment and
self-assertiveness. The old standards based on "God
first, others second, and myself last" do not sound
much like the advice we hear. Who will care for me
if I do not put myself first—especially since I live
alone? But just as Jesus shared with us his body and
blood, so real peace and joy come to us in our sharing
with others even where it may hurt the most.

Teach me, heavenly Father, how to minister to
those about me by unselfish love and sharing.
If there is someone near me today with a special
need, help me to assist you in meeting it. Amen.

Watch in your contacts with others today for a
particularly crabby or unpleasant person. Pray for
him that God may touch his life and cause him to be
"surprised by joy."

■ BOTH WOMEN AND MEN

Matt. 27:45-56:   "There were many women there
. . . who had followed Jesus from Galilee" (v. 55).

A friend who is single commented on her pleasure in an evening for which an invitation had brought her into a group of both women and men. It is especially easy for those who are older and live alone to settle into social patterns that include only that sex of which they are members. All of us need the stimulation of mixed company. Human society to be natural must include both men and women. If we find ourselves with only one group, we need to make an effort to broaden our contacts. Many of us find the variety we seek in our careers, but there are also other groups of people—church, social, political, educational—which provide mixed fellowship.

The group around Jesus was mixed. Besides his disciples, there were also "many women there . . . who had followed Jesus from Galilee." They ministered to Jesus; he—and no doubt his disciples—ministered to them. Some have the mistaken notion spiritual matters are women's affair. But the company of Jesus was made up of both men and women. So it should be among his community, with women and men each ministering to the other.

Prayer Suggestion: Pray for all those who live alone whose situations limit them in their friendships. Pray that congregations develop more sensitivity to the need for a ministry to single people.

Plan an informal, low-cost gathering with a mix of married and single friends just to have a pleasant time together.

■ A TRAGIC KIND OF SINGLENESS

Mark 5:1-20: "He was met by a man who . . . had an evil spirit in him and lived among the tombs" (vv. 2-3).

We live as singles for many reasons, some self-chosen, others not. If not all of us look upon singleness as a gift, at least most of us handle it with adequate poise and competency. But there is a kind of living alone which is the result of mental and emotional disorder. Such a life is illustrated in this story which Mark records for us of the demoniac who lived in the cemetery. His own worst enemy, with his unnatural strength he was unhandleable and lived where others seldom came.

While most people just let him alone, one person appeared on the shores of his life who, even before the demented man had run to him, ordered the demons to come out of him. The result? The isolated and estranged man, clothed in garments someone had shared with him, sat quietly, knowing only that the new desire of his life was to stay with Jesus. Instead, in his home community he became a witness to the power of Christ.

Are there afflicted people in our communities who could be loved back from psychological trauma by those of us to whom Christ offers his presence and power?

Lord, even in our ignorance of how best to help others, cause your healing love to flow through us to their blessing. Amen.

Check into the possibility of your contributing an hour or two a week to a service program staffed by volunteers.

■ THE NEED FOR A RETREAT

Mark 6:30-51:   "Let us go off by ourselves to some place where we will be alone and you can rest a while" (v. 31).

Sometimes as a single with a career, a home to keep clean, clothes to mend and wash, and activities to participate in, I exclaim in frustration, "What I need is a housewife!" The chores and duties that can be shared in a family all seem to be mine, and I am hassled and tired. Yet, when I remember Jesus saying, "Let us go off by ourselves to some place where we will be alone and you can rest awhile," I look around my living place and know that it is as quiet a place as I am likely to find, and no other place is necessarily more restful. If the retreats I have attended are typical, they are often packed with too little silence, too much talking, and too little chance to "rest a while."

Perhaps we who can control the noise around us because we live alone need to discipline ourselves to meditate more, to develop inner quiet and listen for God to speak. Or maybe the kind of retreat we need is a change in setting, the noisy kind of retreat where we can talk in depth with those who share our faith and growth. Then, having rested a while, we go back to be a benediction to a noisy world.

 Prayer Suggestion: Rather than praying in words, simply be quiet before God with eyes closed and hands quiet, letting your mind envision Jesus standing before you with arms outstretched.

Repeat this meditation twice before the day is done. Take time for the experience to be meaningful.

◼ THE HEALTH OF THE BODY

Luke 8:40-48: "My daughter, your faith has made you well. Go in peace" (v. 48).

This woman had spent all her living on doctors. No wonder she sought Jesus' healing touch. Unable to muster courage to approach Jesus openly with her plea to be cured, she reached out to touch the hem of his garment, and she was healed.

Physical illness is a worry for people who live alone, especially as we add on the years. What will we do if we cannot take care of ourselves? How will we live if we should be unable to work or if our support should fail? These questions are serious ones. Worries about health that come during a night when we do not feel well can escalate our symptoms until the flu seems like double pneumonia; an upset stomach convinces us we have cancer; any chest discomfort is quickly labeled a fatal form of heart disease.

Our fears and our imaginings are as often in need of healing as our bodies. When physical health needs the attention of a doctor, we can be grateful for all God has revealed to medical research, and seek help. When the gloom of fear and night activate our imaginations, we need to turn on the light and take a look at God's promises in his Word.

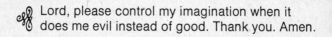 Lord, please control my imagination when it does me evil instead of good. Thank you. Amen.

Arrange with a friend that the two of you can always feel free to call each other, even at night, when you are in need of human reassurance.

■ THE MEAL JESUS SERVED

Luke 9:10-17: "There were about five thousand men there" (v. 14).

M ost often Luke is the writer who records how women were involved in the story of Jesus' life, but in the account of the feeding of the five thousand Matthew is the only one to add "not counting the women and children" to the number of those who had eaten the meal Jesus provided. The omission is not strange: these books were written in a period of history in which women and children were of no great importance.

Women are sometimes called touchy if they react to the presence of sexism in the church. Yet one wonders how men would react if pronouns used in biblical writing were consistently addressed only to women. Of course we know that generic pronouns refer to humans in general. Yet all of us have an innate desire to be included and present in scriptural promises and statements.

Study carefully the portrayal of Jesus. You will find again and again the sensitivity he displays to individuals. The one who lives alone has no need to fear that Jesus will simply issue a statistical count. To him the individual is precious, and a person's sex is not the measure of his or her importance.

Thank you, Lord Jesus, for not lumping us into groups but loving us as individuals. Amen.

Compare the language of liturgy and hymns in a recent hymnal with that of older ones. What changes are intended to eliminate sexism in language?

■ THE INNER STILLNESS

Luke 9:18-27: "And it came to pass, as he was alone praying, his disciples were with him" (v. 18 KJV).

I wonder how many times I had read the verse above before I realized what it was saying: Jesus is praying *alone in the presence of his disciples.* Drawing within himself, he was speaking to his Father. Yet there, within reach, were the men with whom he was spending his days.

We who are single can understand that seeming contradiction of aloneness and togetherness. There are times when we too, even if we are surrounded by other people, withdraw into ourselves to think out problems, ponder decisions, analyze relationships—and pray. Each of us is an individual and must find his or her own identity in moments alone as well as in the fellowship of others.

Developing the inner resources to be content and able to handle our aloneness even in the midst of crowds is important. Then, like our Lord, we can talk things over with the Father in the quietness of our hearts even when others are around us.

My Father, help me to know what it means in my life to pray without ceasing even when others are around me. Teach me to make prayer a part of every situation. Amen.

Look for a specific opportunity today to withdraw alone in the presence of others to pray for some need that is apparent in those about you.

■ SHARING IN THE HARVEST

Luke 10:1-9: "There is a large harvest, but few workers to gather it in" (v. 2).

The gospel writers are so involved in recording the training of the Twelve to carry out Jesus' ministry that we get only glimpses, as in the reading above, of the training of many others. Here Jesus sent seventy to those places where he himself would later go. He asked them to pray to the owner of the harvest for more workers. Out of that prayer down through the centuries of the church have come millions of "harvesters" for the seed of the Word. Many of those who have gone out have been singles, free to come and go as the church called them for its needs at home and abroad.

The vision for mission is much brighter in some parts of the church than in others. The calling and sending of harvesters happens often in some congregations; in others the need is hardly mentioned —especially the need in foreign countries. One can only conclude that even among many who are themselves harvesters, missions have low priority. Christ directed his followers to pray that workers would be sent out. It is up to us to do so, and then to see how we ourselves are called to fit into the harvest.

Father, I pray that you will continue to call out harvesters to reap the fruits of the sowing of the Word. Show me what I can do as part of the harvest crew. Amen.

Find out how many pastors and missionaries have been called from the membership of your congregation in its history. Pray accordingly.

■ A VISIT TO BETHANY

Luke 10:38-42: "Jesus . . . came to a village where a woman named Martha welcomed him in her home" (v. 38).

From what we are told in the Gospels, we understand that Mary, Martha, and Lazarus were a household of singles. How natural that Jesus should find that home one to which he loved to come! No doubt some of the disciples, being younger than their teacher, were also single. Here in this Bethany home they could relax together. Here was a group of single friends being supportive of each other with love and concern. Here each could be accepted for himself or herself. Each could hear with wonderment the words of Jesus as he shared his wisdom with them, and Mary, who forsook everything else to listen, could be commended for having "chosen the right thing."

As singles we can envision ourselves part of that circle. We too need a circle of supportive friends and have a responsibility to be such a friend to others. One thing we have in common with Mary and Martha and Lazarus: God's Word tells us that he loves us too.

Prayer Suggestions: Pray today for: 1) your friends who live alone that they may learn contentment in their life situations, 2) those who are supportive of you—both married and single ones, 3) those who in their singleness work where they are often lonely, and 4) yourself, that you may be a nourishing friend to others.

Call a friend who has meant especially much to you in your Christian life and let him or her know how much you appreciate the friendship.

■ TO OPEN AND TO SHUT

Luke 11:1-3: "Don't bother me! The door is already locked" (v. 7).

One privilege that those of us who live alone have is that of closing the door behind us. Are we aware of how many others do not have that privilege? Consider, for instance, the nurse who comes home from her 7:00 A.M. to 3:00 P.M. shift just as her children come home from school, or the man who comes home just in time for the furor of the evening meal. No matter how tired either is, the door cannot be shut on the demands of others. Singles can choose, at least much of the time, to shut the door, but we do not always appreciate this built-in benefit of living alone.

Yet there is another side to that benefit. When others in need, like the man in our text, come to us for help, the door must be opened again. We have not only ourselves to consider. There are times when we may decide the door must remain shut because we need to gather strength if we are to be able to give again. But more often the door must be open to someone's need. God, by his Spirit's guidance, will help us to know the one time from the other.

Lord, if I am keeping my door shut when it should be open to another's need, give me the urge to open it. Amen.

Take a look at your outside door. Does it present a neat, attractive appearance to those who come to see you?

■ KEEPING HOLIDAY

Luke 14:12-24: "How happy are those who will sit down at the feast in the Kingdom of God" (v. 15).

The most festive days for families are often the loneliest days for many who live alone. Christmas, Easter, the Fourth of July, birthdays—these occasions for family gatherings can be long and dreary days for those with no families or whose families do not include them in their celebrations. Worst off are those who always wait for someone else to take the initiative in planning an interesting day. Often such people have negative self-images and assume that no one would care to spend even part of a festive day with them.

If those of us who are plagued with such problems and attitudes could only realize we are not that different from others. As we sit waiting for someone to invite us to come closer, someone else also waits, yearning to be approached. Often both sit alone. This need not be. Moreover, the joy of a celebration is greater for those who extend hospitality to someone who otherwise would be left out than for those who invite only those who can repay the invitation. Jesus warned us against including others on the basis of who can repay us. The most God-pleasing invitations go to those who need us rather than to those who reward us.

Remind me, Lord, when I should be reaching out to people in ways that can ease their loneliness on some special day. Amen.

Find out the birthdays of five people who live alone. Keep them where you will see them to remind yourself to give them a birthday call.

■ HANDLING YOUR POSSESSIONS

Luke 16:1-13:   "If, then, you have not been faithful in handling worldly wealth, how can you be trusted with true wealth?" (v. 11).

Faithfulness in handling worldly wealth may not seem a great problem in a day of inflation when almost all our income goes for what we see as necessities. But the question Jesus asks here causes us to examine the central allegiance of our hearts.

Perhaps we have never thought of this text as having anything to do with making a will. For a believer who lives as a single, a will is a vital part of making sure that the part of our estate which could go to support causes we have believed in does not go primarily to the state in inheritance taxes. A will should be made early in life and revised as circumstances in our lives alter. Most church bodies have brochures available that give excellent information on handling one's estate. Our money invested in the church can both produce income for us and enable the church to keep serving in our name.

We are stewards of what God has given us. We should be intelligent and informed stewards, by our faithfulness enabling the work of the kingdom to be maintained and expanded.

 Lord, help me to find joy and fulfillment in being an intelligent supporter of the work of the kingdom. Amen.

Call your church office and ask to be supplied with your church body's brochures on estate planning.

■ FAITH IN TOMORROW

Luke 21:25-38: "Be on watch and pray always . . ."
(v. 36).

The years my life has spanned have never been boring. I have been aware of economic catastrophe and drought; my college classmates went off to and came home from war; my students went off—or refused to go off—to Vietnam. When I visited Finland a few years after World War II, a beautiful young woman told me that thousands of Finnish girls did not expect to marry—so many men had died in the war.

Almost every age of human history has been tragedy-ridden. Plagues swept through cities and decimated populations; earthquakes and storm took their toll; always there was war somewhere. Yet human life has known much of joy and beauty too. The future will be as bright as the promises of God. "Stand up and raise your heads," said Jesus. Today is a good time in many ways for people who live alone; the future for us is brighter yet. "We don't know what the future holds, but we know who holds the future."

 When my heart is full of foreboding about the future, dear Lord, help me to remember that you hold it in your hands. Amen.

Take time to list four predictions of disaster that did not come true.

COMPANY AT MEALTIME

Luke 24:13-35: "The two then explained to them what had happened on the road, and how they had recognized the Lord when he broke the bread" (v. 35).

Prayer before meals can become a dull, routine exercise. Meals themselves can be dull if we let them —they sometimes are in spite of our attempts to prevent it. Spending much time and effort in the preparation of food for one person seems excessive. The meal often does not move from the counter to the table. Even if it does, many of us read our way through it, or watch television. The numbers of singles eating in restaurants is evidence that many of us have sought companionship at the mealtime hour by going out to eat. Yet that too can become routine-ridden, with limited choices and too much expense.

The disciples at Emmaus came to recognize Jesus in the breaking of the bread. Surely that happens in the Eucharist. But the meal at Emmaus was an ordinary meal. Can we too recognize that we never really eat alone, that the Christ who made himself known that evening on the road to Emmaus is close to us in the breaking of our bread? In his presence it is worth setting our table with our prettiest dishes (who are we saving them for anyway?) and well-planned food. Our prayers and our meals can be loving conversations with the one who makes himself known in the breaking of the bread.

Prayer Suggestion: Take time to pray for the hungry people of the world—and for those who have much but share little with others.

Put away some of the everyday dishes you have been using and brighten your meals by using some of your "good" dishes.

■ THE ROLE OF ANNOUNCER

John 1:35-46:   "The two disciples heard him say this and went with Jesus" (v. 37).

One of the famous singles of the Bible is John the Baptist. While we are not specifically told that he did not marry, we see that his life-style could hardly have included a wife. John's life seems a lonely and difficult one. We hope that in his youth he spent many enjoyable hours with his cousin Jesus, just six months younger. But we know little of the youth of either one of them.

When John came out of the desert to be the voice crying in the wilderness, disciples joined themselves to him. These disciples saw John point to Jesus as the "Lamb of God, who takes away the sin of the world." Some of them changed their allegiance from John to Jesus. They heard John speak, but they followed Jesus.

What happens to those who hear us speak of our beliefs? Are they, like those who heard John, inspired to follow Jesus? Do we convince other people that Jesus is the ideal companion and friend, worthy of their allegiance and service? Are we "John" in someone's life, pointing not at ourselves but at Christ?

Lord, grant that when people hear me speak, they may be drawn to you. Amen.

Look for an opportunity today to simply and naturally tell someone how grateful you are for Christ in your life.

■ THE UNCONDEMNING CHRIST

John 8:1-11: "I do not condemn you either. Go, but do not sin again" (v. 11).

Many of the millions of us who live alone know what it is like to feel condemned for our life-style by others. While many of us have chosen to live alone for personal or career reasons, some have been left alone by broken marriages or by estrangement, by quarrels in families, by suspicion of disapproved sexual behavior. Such aloneness is more likely to be beset by loneliness. The feeling that others condemn us for our situation in life can wall us in, suppress our enjoyment of life, dampen our initiative when we most need to exercise it. All this even when we know that those who condemn us are themselves imperfect.

The one who knows us more fully even than we know ourselves does not condemn us. Though he knows better than we what fault is in us, he forgives. "If our conscience condemns us, we know that God is greater than our conscience and that he knows everything" (1 John 3:20), even our despair over the condemnation of others. "There is no condemnation now for those who live in union with Christ Jesus" (Rom. 8:1). In Christ is where we were put by our baptism, and we are always welcome there.

 Prayer Suggestion: Praise God in your own words because his forgiveness, beyond our imagining, is so much more available than that of others—and even our own.

Memorize the following sentence: No matter how great my sins may be, they are never greater than God's love and forgiveness.

■ THE PERSONAL TOUCH

John 13:1-15: "You, then, should wash one
another's feet" (v. 14).

I once heard a man serving in a healing ministry
say, "There are people here tonight who could be
healed if someone would just *touch* them." I assume
he was talking about psychological healing, about
meeting the needs aroused by the isolation and
loneliness such as that which many people who live
alone feel.

The custom of foot-washing has become rare in
Christian circles in spite of Jesus' recommendation
of it. No doubt there are many reasons. Shoes have
replaced sandals; groups of believers are often large,
and many people are almost strangers to one another.
There are other ways of serving each other.

I hope its demise is not related to our reluctance
in our society to touch each other, to the fact that to
many such contact would be distasteful as well as hard
on their pride. So many need to be touched with love
as the motivating force, to be assured by our touch
that they are worth being loved, that they belong in
the family of those whom God loves. Just as power
went out from Jesus to the woman who had touched
the hem of his garment, a healing reassurance of love
can flow from us to others in our touch.

Lord, make me a toucher through whom your love
can flow to heal and encourage. Amen.

**Keep your eyes open today for an opportunity to
touch with love someone who is in need of reassurance.**

■ THE INESCAPABLE DECISION

John 21:15-23:   "If I want him to live until I come, what is that to you? Follow me!" (v. 22).

A happily married person and a self-sufficient single person are both individuals whose well-being is dependent not on losing their individuality to someone else but in exploring with others in warm human relationships what they are and can be. When Peter, mourning his disloyalty to his Lord, found it hard to handle what Jesus predicted for his future, he turned his attention to what would happen to John, that beloved younger disciple who had done better than Peter in following Jesus through the horrible weekend of the crucifixion. "Lord, what about this man?" But Jesus would not let Peter's attention waver. "What is that to you? Follow me."

It is as myself, an individual, that I make my decision to follow, not as a member of a family or a partner in a marriage. Everyone else aside, I decide to follow. *Then* the family of God supports me and I find in it the nourishing friendships that, as one who has social as well as individual needs, give me support and joy.

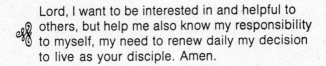

Lord, I want to be interested in and helpful to others, but help me also know my responsibility to myself, my need to renew daily my decision to live as your disciple. Amen.

Set aside a period of time today to take a careful look at the direction of your own life: where you have been, where you are, and where you are going. Does this suggest any action you should be taking?

■ NOT EXEMPTION BUT EMPOWERING

Rom. 8:26-32: "We know that in all things God works for good with those who love him" (v. 28).

An idea often present in Old Testament times was that believers were exempt from the dangers and catastrophes that plagued others. Psalm 91, for example, assumes that plagues and even death in war happen only to those who do not abide in God. Yet we see again and again that this is not so—God's people are not exempt from the troubles of life. Only one of Jesus' disciples escaped a martyr's death.

We who live as singles are often aware of dangers against which we must guard. In many places we are cautioned not to walk alone, to have adequate locks on our doors and windows, to be suspicious of strangers. To be a believer is not to be automatically safe from what threatens others, so these precautions are ones we should heed.

But we are assured that whatever happens, hard though it may be to understand, is ultimately for our spiritual good. That does not mean we should throw caution to the winds, but it does mean that even when threatened we may know a great peace.

Father, give me the trust I need to believe that in everything you work for my good. Amen.

Take a moment to answer these questions. Act on any you answer negatively. 1. Do I carry money in a sensible, not-obvious way? 2. Do my doors and windows have adequate locks which I use regularly? 3. Do the routes of my daily journeyings needlessly expose me to danger? 4. Is my living place as accident-proof as I can make it?

■ APPRECIATING OUR DIFFERENCES

Rom. 12:1-8: "We have many parts in the one body, and all these parts have different functions" (v. 4).

Paul is speaking in this passage about the body of Christ, the church, and its need for people to fill a diversity of functions. He is using a symbol, that of a body with many organs, which can also be applied to a circle of friends. That circle is most satisfying to us if it has variety, if the diverse needs for friendship in our lives are all cared for. A group of overly similar people may lack the spice and stimulation friendship needs.

Most of us likely choose our friends spontaneously and without premeditation; fortunately variety usually takes care of itself. Some are constant givers, others always takers. Some initiate social contacts, others seldom do. Some actively cherish friendships, others coast along and assume them. Some are openly affectionate and touchers, others are reserved and undemonstrative. As people who live alone, we can rejoice if our friends bring variety into our lives. We can also rejoice that "some friends are more loyal than brothers" (Prov. 18:24) and that Jesus is one such friend.

 Thank you, Lord, for my friends. Thank you too that my richest experience of friendship can be my relationship with you. Amen.

Analyze yourself as a friend according to the descriptive statements in paragraph 2 above. Where do you fit?

■ THE PEACEABLE LIFE

Rom. 12:9-21: "Do everything possible on your part to live in peace with everybody" (v. 18).

One of the pleasures of heaven will be getting to know St. Paul. He was a man very knowledgeable about human nature, as evidenced by the phrase "on your part" in the verse above. Looking at his life from conversion to martyrdom, we recognize why he added that clause. During much of his life he was embroiled in religious and legal conflict. Much of it resulted from events over which he had no control.

We will usually have to admit in our daily lives, though, that living peaceably with others is largely in our hands. Wisdom and tact for this grow out of the Spirit's work within us. We don't need the tensions and headaches and upset stomachs that result from holding on to grudges that develop when anger is nourished and cherished. Those of us who live alone can spend too much time nursing disagreements into hostilities. It is vital to "do everything possible . . . to live in peace with everybody."

 Lord, make me one of your blessed peacemakers who will be numbered among the children of God. Amen.

Watch for an opportunity today to calm a moment of stress that threatens the peace among those with whom you work.

■ THE BODY FOR THE LORD

1 Cor. 6:12-20:   "The body is not to be used for sexual immorality, but to serve the Lord" (v. 13).

One of the most common arguments used by women advocating the legal and moral right to abortion is that a woman's body belongs to her. While we understand what they mean, we know too, if we are believers, that our bodies do not belong ultimately to us. As Paul puts it, "The body is to serve the Lord." An interview with a former Miss America quoted her as saying she was opposed to drinking and smoking because her body was God's temple, but in almost the next sentence she favored free choice of abortion since a woman's body was her own. We humans are not always logical.

The person who lives as a single and believes that his or her body is to be used "to serve the Lord" can face much outside pressure and many inner problems in relation to sexuality. This is especially true in a society so obsessed with sex as ours. God's Word is clear on his standards. Church history has abundant evidence that the energies spent on sex in marriage can be sublimated for use in God's service and service to others. Christians down through history have not always done equally well in being understanding of those singles who find this a difficult area of life to handle.

 Lord, will you who designed our bodies help us to use them in our individual situations in ways pleasing to you? Amen.

Read Matthew 7:1-5 as a reminder for the day.

■ THE COMFORT OF OUR PRESENCE

2 Cor. 1:3-7:   "He helps us in all our troubles,
so that we are able to help others who have all
kinds of troubles" (v. 4).

I have often found that the greatest comfort in a
time of need is not in many words poured into the
situation but is instead in the presence of a person
who takes time to be with me. While that is likely true
for everyone, it is even more true for those of us who
live alone who need in our difficult moments to have
a human presence with us. The person who says in a
time of sorrow or disgrace or illness, "I would go to see
him but I never know what to say," is missing the
point. What we say may be trite or fresh, brief or
lengthy, profound or trivial. What matters is that we
go and show we care.

Few of us have a more valuable gift than our time
to give. Time is hard to stretch, and that time which we
share is gone from our day. But in exchange we have
a joy, a sense that we have shared what matters, what
is truly ours to give. This God does when he assures
us of his presence with us, not with words but with
an abundance of love.

Lord, I am grateful for the comfort you and
others have given in my times of need. Help me
to be an effective comforter in the needs of
others. Amen.

**Take a moment to address and send the note of
sympathy or encouragement you have been meaning
to get at for some days now.**

■ SPREADING HIS FRAGRANCE

2 Cor. 2:12-17:   "God uses us to make the knowledge about Christ spread everywhere like a sweet fragrance" (v. 14).

I can remember from my youth the prevalence of the idea that single women, "old maids" as they were called when past some never-really-defined age, were frustrated, inhibited, and eccentric. With that kind of attitude toward them common in society, it was a wonder if they were not. Bachelors, no doubt, had a similar problem to face, though not to the degree their single sisters did.

Fortunately social attitudes can change, and in most places now we are not so quick to stereotype or be stereotyped. Paul in our text suggests that as Christians we build up a different kind of stereotype to be recognized wherever we go—that of people who "make the knowledge about Christ spread everywhere like a sweet fragrance."

What fragrance permeates the church we belong to? What fragrance fills the air of our apartments or houses? Is there a poisonous air of suspicion, self-centeredness, criticism? Or is there an atmosphere of love, acceptance, openness, warmth, and poise because we have the knowledge of God? Does it move others to say, "He (or she) must be one of those people called Christians"?

Lord, may the fragrance of my knowledge of you be evident to others in my work, my home, and my church. Amen.

Put one of your containers of cologne on a shelf by your sink to remind you daily that your life should give off the fragrance of God's love.

■ OLD WALLS BROKEN DOWN

Gal. 3:21-29: "So there is no difference between Jews and Gentiles, between slaves and free men, between men and women; you are all one in union with Christ Jesus" (v. 28).

Something there is that doesn't love a wall, that wants it down," says Robert Frost. Looking from another direction, we could say that we humans are constant wall-builders. We fashion walls out of almost every available difference between people—age, sex, creed, race. We build them so sturdily it takes centuries to knock them down. Even those walls broken down by our being one in Christ have a way of tripping us up on their ruins.

Forces fearful of change within the church have sturdily fought to shore up the walls broken down by Paul's proclamation that "there is no difference . . . between men and women" in Christ Jesus. Woman, they say, is to find her identity and duty in relation to her husband. What does one do with the single woman in a system like that? She is somehow left out of the pattern, as the single man is left out of the requirement that he be the head of his wife.

Maybe singles have the best opportunity of all to explore what it means to "submit yourselves to one another because of your reverence for Christ" (Eph. 5:21). Maybe we are in the best position to tear down old walls that in Christ should be done away with but which human nature has preserved.

Lord, help us not to see in our freedom an excuse for refusing to consider the welfare of others as carefully as our own. Amen.

Search to discover what harmful walls you are preserving within yourself. Plan some change that will effectively knock them down for good.

■ NO LONGER STRANGERS

Ephesians 2: ". . . you are now fellow citizens with God's people and members of the family of God" (v. 19).

If only every congregation could apply the idea of "family" to its church life. Some do—they are warm, loving families of believers in which all are at home and accepted. In churches which practice the sharing of the peace in the service, some congregations are spontaneous, accepting, open; others are stilted and reserved. It is obvious that some do not value community.

If I were, after all these years in one congregation, to choose another church home, I would want to watch that congregation share the peace. I would want to know, as someone who lives alone, if I could find a family in that congregation. For individuals to come and go from a service and greet no one is sad. They neither add to nor draw from the fund of love which the family has for each other.

I need that family. That obligates me to it. If I am unconcerned that others feel the family's acceptance and warmth, I will find little of that warmth myself. In 3 John, the author tells Gaius, "My dear friend, you are so faithful in the work you do for your fellow Christians, even when they are strangers" (v. 5). Be sure to greet the family!

 Lord, help both me and the congregation to which I belong to be open channels through which your love flows to others. Amen.

Some of the love for the family should flow to our pastors and their families. Do something today to express your warmth toward them.

■ DO EVEN MORE

1 Thess. 4:1-12: "You yourselves have been taught by God how you should love one another. . . . Do even more" (vv. 9, 10).

Loving is not something we automatically know how to do. We learn how to love or we do not learn how to love, depending on our early experiences with parents and others. Happy is the baby who is loved: that child will learn how to love in return. Paul, commending the Christians at Thessalonica who have learned from God how to love, challenges them to do even more of that loving in their relationships with other Christians.

No doubt some people live as singles because they have not learned enough about how to love others. Through the years they have found it easier to get along with themselves than to adapt themselves to life lived intimately with others. Thus we limit our lives and our egos grow as fragile as the eggshell of a chicken with no calcium. Unless others are exactly what we think they should be, we see them as being wrong and reject fellowship with them.

All of us need constantly to be taught by God to love others—and all of us need to be challenged to "do even more." As that great Calvary love of God is accepted into our lives, we are enabled to reach out to love others—even more.

 Prayer Suggestion: Take time to pray in your own words for three people you sense have difficulty in loving and accepting others. Pray that by showing your love to them, you may be used to set them free to love.

Give one of these three a cheering telephone call today, assuring them of your concern and love for them.

■ AN IMPOSSIBLE REQUEST?

1 Thess. 5:9-24: " . . . be thankful in all circumstances" (v. 18).

In everything give thanks? Is that an impossible dream, or is it for the Christian a realizable achievement?

—to give thanks for living as a single because of the avenues that opens for me to develop and grow as an individual?

—to give thanks for the need to economize that I may develop a truer sense of values, a better order of priorities?

—to be thankful for a handicap of one of my senses that I may develop a greater sensitivity in the others?

—to be thankful for a health problem that increases my appreciation for the days when I feel really good, or for just being alive?

—to be thankful to be a member of a congregation that is imperfect because that is the only kind where I would fit?

—to be thankful for imperfect friends for the same reason?

—to be thankful when my home seems too quiet because I can more intently listen for the voice of God in my heart?

—to be thankful at the death of a friend in spite of grief because I believe that God is working some unseen good through it?

—to be thankful for pain because of the sympathy and understanding that it can give me for others who suffer?

Lord, I know I can "be thankful in all circumstances" only by your help. Thank you that it is available. Amen.

Add five items of your own to the list above.

■ THE PRIVILEGE OF PRAYER

2 Thess. 2:13—3:5:   "Finally, our brothers, pray for us" (3:1).

A colleague of mine has a habit of assuring anyone with a problem that she will do some "knee-work" for them. Though she wears a nun's veil, no sceptic or Protestant ever fails to respond to the concern her offer to pray for their need shows.

If we have any question about what we can do as ministry to and for others in our daily lives, her example suggests an answer. Is the bus driver crabby this morning? Pray that something beautiful will touch his life as the day goes on. Is the waitress red-eyed and sad? As you pay her, tell her God loves her. Is your employer curt with her husband on the telephone? Pray that God will strengthen and bless their relationship. Is a child on the sidewalk in tears? Maybe he needs a hug and a prayer.

We know little about how spiritual influences operate between human beings. But we do know that what is positive and loving is evident and others respond; what is hostile and negative creates its own kind of vibrations. We can leave an invisible trail of blessing behind us through the day if we constantly lift others up for God to touch them with his benediction.

Suggestion for Prayer: Think ahead into your day and pray for the people you know you will meet. Ask the Holy Spirit to show you how to pray for those around you who have special needs.

Make yourself a little sign that asks "Whom did I bless by my prayers today?" and keep it by the clock on your bed table.

■ THE DISCIPLINE OF A GODLY LIFE

1 Timothy 4: "Keep yourself in training for a
godly life" (v. 7).

A godly life" is one of those biblical phrases that
to many today sounds archaic, as if one had notions
of being a religious fanatic. We Christians are told
from all directions that our lives need not look
different because of the faith we profess. "We're OK;
you're OK." Relax. That is all God or others expect.

A speaker I once heard imagined Jesus looking
down from the cross at the people around him and
saying, "If I'm OK and you're OK, then what in the
name of God am I doing on this cross?" Jesus, with his
forty days and nights in the wilderness and his many
nights of prayer, knows what training for a godly
life means.

How can we who live alone structure our daily
routine to include training for a godly life? It will
mean "reporting in" for his service in the morning and
closing the day with gratitude for his help, as well as
constant response to his Spirit's guidance during the
day. The number of popularity polls or prestigious
elections we win will not count. What will count is
being sensitive to what he has told us of his will
and his work in our relationships with others.

Prayer Suggestion: A godly life might seem a
rather frightening goal. Pray that God will reveal
exactly what this means for you.

Check the meaning of "godly" in a dictionary. If you
have a concordance, trace down other passages in the
New Testament that talk about a godly life. What
does it really involve?

■ THE FAMILY OF FAITH

1 Tim. 5:1-16: "Treat the younger men as your brothers, the older women as mothers, and the younger women as sisters, with all purity" (vv. 1, 2).

Quite often I worship Sunday mornings with a university campus congregation which I much enjoy. It has only one "flaw"—except for a few stray faculty like me and a parent or two almost all the people are the same age. The family of God includes all ages. Paul, advising the young pastor Timothy how to relate to his congregation, reminds him of the family structure of the congregation.

As we choose our friends and companions, those of us who live as singles benefit from the variety of ages and backgrounds we include. A child or two helps us stay young. Biological grandparents are never enough—we need to add a few from our immediate surroundings. Young people share with us their plans and enthusiasms. Middle-aged people add stability and a settled feeling. If any of these are missing, we need to find and add them.

The family of God's children is our family out of spiritual kinship. Many of us have several "adopted families" we look on as our own, giving us the opportunity to share with and rejoice in their experiences too. The family of God has infinite variety.

 Prayer Suggestion: Pray for those who are your "family," with whom you share those things that belong to family closeness.

Take a step today toward getting to know an older person who lives near you. Is he or she someone you could add to your family?

■ THE CHOICE OF LIFE-STYLE

1 Tim. 6:1-16: "If we have food and clothes, that should be enough for us" (v. 8).

More and more often today we are being called on to look at our life-styles to see if they are showing the necessary stewardship and concern for natural resources, the Christian willingness to share with others in this world the food and fiber they too need. We as singles have a peculiar opportunity to adapt our life-styles to the world's needs. We buy and cook and plan for ourselves. It should be more possible for us to live simply, to avoid waste, to so order our days that we can avoid conspicuous consumption. There can be just as much satisfaction—even more—in denying ourselves unneeded luxuries than in always giving in to our desires. In that way we leave more of the earth's resources for others. We need to think through carefully the dichotomy suggested in the book title *Rich Christians in an Age of Hunger*. Riches of the kind Thoreau suggests are numerous: "I am rich in the number of things I can do without."

"I am going to make sure I get my share and more" is not a Christian attitude. God does not ask us to be niggardly, to live narrow cramped lives, but he does ask us to live by priorities set by love.

 Help me, O Lord, to be able to sort out those things necessary to my life and happiness from those without which I could be just as content. Grant me the grace of simplicity in my daily life. Amen.

Decide on one change you can make today to simplify your life-style. Try it out.

■ THE COMFORT OF KINDNESS

Titus 3:1-8: "Tell them not to speak evil of anyone, . . . and always to show a gentle attitude toward everyone" (v. 2).

W orking in the teaching profession, where people tend to speak their minds quite frankly, I needed to be taught by my students how important gentleness can be. I still remember my shock when a young wife told me that her student husband, a veteran, was so upset by having forgotten an appointment with one of my colleagues that he actually became sick to his stomach. He did not expect gentle treatment for a very human act of forgetfulness. That incident stopped my tongue many times—though probably not as often as it should have.

Gentleness in families is crucial, but we who live alone also need to remember, in our contacts with friends and acquaintances, what fragility exists in the human ego. We can raise someone's spirits for a whole day by being gently understanding when something goes wrong. Conversely, we can dash the spirits of even a complete stranger by a blunt and harsh remark in his or her presence. No wonder Paul lists gentleness as one of the fruits of the Spirit—it is a fruit which brings the fragrance of God into a situation. People who lack this quality in their speech often seem unable to realize why others avoid their presence.

Thank you, heavenly Father, for the gentleness with which you have treated me. Help me to be gentle with others. Amen.

Examine your routine associations with friends and coworkers. Is there someone who tests your ability to remain gentle? Try to improve that relationship.

■ A PLACE TO LIVE

Philemon: " . . . get a room ready for me" (v. 22).

Not too many years ago a hiring official I know of recommended a lower salary for a single woman on the grounds that all she would need for housing would be a room. Shades of past attitudes! But housing is often a major concern for people who live alone.

Jesus said of himself that the Son of man had no place to lay his head. Paul, constantly on the move or, for long periods of his life, in prison, seems often to have stayed with other believers such as Prisca and Aquila. In our reading for today he asks Philemon for hospitality. Often Christian singles have found homes in religious orders, mission homes, and within their own families in addition to living independently.

Today we who live as singles often have apartments and even houses of our own, enjoying the privacy and comfort they give us. We are fortunate to live in a time with a healthier recognition of the emotional and economic needs of those who live alone. The place where we live can be the setting for our service to others and our ministry to their needs as well as our own.

Thank you, Lord, for my living place. Make it truly a base where I find refreshment so I can more effectively do my work and share with others. Amen.

Bring out a special item you have stored away to enjoy it as an expression of your appreciation for the place you live.

■ BUT GROW!

Heb. 5:11—6:12: "Let us go forward, then, to mature teaching and leave behind us the first lessons of the Christian message" (6:1).

If only we Christians would be as concerned about our spiritual growth as we are about a child's physical or intellectual growth! The author of Hebrews finds the people to whom he writes slow to learn, old enough in the faith to be teachers of others, yet retarded in the faith to such a degree that they have never gotten past "the first lessons of God's message." Able only to absorb milk, they cannot handle the solid food they need to grow spiritually stronger.

Growth occurs in sharing and interacting with others as well as in our private study and prayer. We who live alone need to seek out the experience of growth that comes from talking about spiritual things with others, from sharing what we have found in our private reading and thought. Not to grow is to die. Not to grow deeper in our knowledge of God and his ways with us is to shrivel and grow weak in our spiritual experience. This need not happen, for he yearns to nourish our faith and growth.

Lord, help me to be constantly growing in faith and knowledge of you. Grant that I may enable others to grow by sharing with them both the milk and the solid food of life in you. Amen.

Find an occasion today to share with a friend something you have read that has stimulated your thinking. Become a "clipper," sharing precious tidbits from your reading with others.

■ A CLOUD OF WITNESSES

Heb. 11:32—12:2: "We have this large crowd of witnesses around us. So then, let us rid ourselves of everything that gets in the way, and of the sin which holds on to us so tightly" (12:1).

We who live alone do many things alone—we open our eyes to a new day, eat, open our mail, shop for groceries, decide what radio station to listen to, pay our taxes, and retire, often with only ourselves for company. Is the author of Hebrews excluding us when he writes of the crowd of witnesses whose surveillance inspires us to "rid ourselves of everything that gets in the way, and of the sin which holds on to us so tightly"?

As Christians we live with that crowd of witnesses from the past looking over our shoulders, with the family of faith about us as we journey, with Jesus, the one "on whom our faith depends" going before us to lead us. Revelation 4 and 21 give us a word picture of the scene there will be when all of these are at last together, and it is as if the words cannot be expanded to hold all the glory and the jubilation that will be part of that time.

To be part of that is incentive to lay aside the hindrances and the pet sins, to run the race laid out before us. Spiritual jogging requires discipline as does physical jogging that we may acquit ourselves well before that crowd of witnesses. Yet when we do, we will still know that our acceptance will be entirely by grace.

Help me to live, dear Lord, aware of those who watch my life to see that I follow the one "on whom our faith depends." Amen.

Read Revelation 4 and 21 today, using your imagination to visualize the scenes being described.

■ ANGELS UNAWARES

Heb. 13:1-8: "Keep on loving one another as Christian brothers. Remember to welcome strangers in your homes. There were some who did that and welcomed angels without knowing it" (vv. 1-2).

O ne of the most frustrating aspects of life is the limited opportunity even the most gregarious person has to become acquainted with more than a few of the fascinating people this world holds. Yet it is so easy to become bound in a routine in which we see the same people over and over, only rarely becoming acquainted with others.

God himself must be a lover of variety—he caused so much of it to exist. We, on the other hand, often seek out as friends only those who are like ourselves. As people living as singles, what opportunity is ours to break the routine, to take up a new activity, to enroll for a course that interests us—all enabling us to meet new people. If we have a hospitable heart, we will welcome the chance to become acquainted with these strangers. Indeed, we may welcome angels without knowing it. God's hospitality in sharing his love and home with us will be reflected in our lives to our joy and enrichment.

 Give me, O Lord, an adventurous spirit in seeking out others who are also your children. Free me from inhibitions in reaching out to them. Amen.

When an opportunity arises today, strike up a conversation with someone you do not know. Show a sincere interest in him or her as a person.

■ THE TEMPTATION OF GOSSIP

James 3: "The tongue is . . . a world of wrong,
occupying its place in our bodies" (v. 6).

Singles down through the ages have had to endure
more than the usual amount of gossip. Given society's
attitude that the single state was abnormal, to be
avoided at almost any cost, it was probably not
strange that idle tongues did not leave the single
person alone. Gossip is, at best, a sort of guessing at
each other; at worst, a venomous attack. Knowing
how readily our behavior is attacked, how quickly we
can be fitted into a stereotype, we need to use our
tongues with care. Truly, "the tongue: small as it is,
. . . can boast about great things." A person's reputation
can so easily be set ablaze with careless words.

But the tongue that "can boast about great things"
can be used for good. All of us, and certainly we who
live alone, need the kind, supportive words of those
about us. We need to be quick to give honest praise,
to encourage, to support someone's sagging morale.

Three questions can guide us in what we say about
each other: Is it true? Is it kind? Is it necessary? Our
silence at times may be the greatest support we can
offer someone when we are invited to join
the gossipers.

O Lord, may my speech sow a harvest of
righteousness both for myself and others. Amen.

**Watch for an opportunity today to squelch an item of
gossip by your silence or by your finding something
to praise in the person under attack.**

■ THE SHARING OF BURDENS

James 5:1-16: "So then, confess your sins to one another and pray for one another, so that you will be healed" (v. 16).

Have we lost something valuable in our neglect of the rite of private confession? True, it would be easy to turn it into a mechanical rite with empty words. True, the act would mean little unless it were voluntary. And yes, the more serious the sin, the harder it would be to confess it to another; the more trivial, the easier to recite routinely. But without such a practice, many who need the reassurance of God's grace and forgiveness spoken directly to them never experience it. C. S. Lewis was a non-Catholic who found it helpful to have a confessor. I am glad my home congregation still practiced individual absolution at least occasionally in connection with the Eucharist. Jesus himself said to those who would lead his church, "What you prohibit on earth shall be prohibited in heaven, and what you permit on earth shall be permitted in heaven" (Matt. 16:19).

Perhaps there are many who feel no need of such a recourse. The person who lives as a single needs to be aware, though, of the need to avoid bearing problems of guilt and trauma that could be relieved by confiding in an understanding Christian pastor or friend. Such a person can speak the needed reassurance of forgiveness and grace.

 Help us, O God of grace, to be for each other the help and reassurance that we as faulty human beings need. Amen.

Use your church or public library to find what the position of your church body is on private confession. Talk it over with a Christian friend.

■ THE QUESTION OF SUBMISSIVENESS

1 Peter 2:13-25:   "You servants must submit
yourselves to your masters and show them
complete respect" (v. 18).

Submissiveness is not a popular word in our society.
We are encouraged to be assertive rather than
submissive, to seek our fulfillment as individuals rather
than subordinate ourselves to anyone. Women today,
having traditionally been advised to be submissive, are
often resentful of any request to be submissive to
men, whether in the family or in the business
world. The majority of singles are women, some of
whom are single because they resent the demand to be
submissive. As singles, they meet this demand
less often.

Like any religion, Christianity is to a degree tied to
the culture within which it exists. In New Testament
times and for centuries after, women had little choice
except to be subject to father, brother, or husband.
Women today are more independent. But no matter
what our role in relation to those of the other sex, the
Christian principle of "God first, others second, self
third" offers more lasting satisfaction than the very
human and very modern "Self first, others when they
help me fulfill myself, and God when he comes
in handy."

> Lord, it is so easy to assume that putting myself
> first will create happiness. Help me know the
> truth and to understand what your Word says
> about this human tendency. Amen.

**Take some time to examine in your mind the example
of a friend who seems able to blend self-confident
independence and Christian submissiveness gracefully.
What seems to be his or her secret?**

■ THE PRECIOUSNESS OF BAPTISM

1 Peter 3:13-22: "Baptism . . . now saves you" (v. 21).

A statement that recently struck deep in my memory was one by Sister Maria José Hobday: "I am washed all my life long in the waters of my baptism." That does not mean baptism is some sort of magic rite. It is a sacrament underwritten by God's word and promise, unfailing and unending.

Baptism has two aspects, both of them meaningful for us as singles. It is a corporate event: in it I become a part of a family, one of the people of God, a member of a community of faith. I can never again be truly alone. It is also an individual event: God accepts me as a daughter or son, his child. I can never again be without a father. As an individual I am of worth because he has accepted me.

It is possible for me by my choice or by my neglect to walk away from what baptism gives me. But God will never walk away from his promise to me given in my baptism. That baptism connects me to the death and resurrection of Jesus Christ, and that will never lose its power.

 Prayer Suggestion: In your prayer, give thanks 1) for those who were responsible for your baptism, 2) for the faithful promises of God to you in baptism, and 3) for the assurance that you can walk secure in the covenant of your baptism.

Find your baptismal certificate and read it again. Ask someone who was present to tell you about your baptismal day.